Bill,

With God's blessings.

Patrick J. Sena Cssr

Nov 2, 1985

1

THE APOCALYPSE

Biblical Revelation Explained

ACKNOWLEDGMENT: Biblical quotations used throughout this work are from the Revised Standard Version, used with permission.

To all those to whom
I have had the privilege
of teaching B417,
Understanding the Apocalypse.

THE APOCALYPSE

Biblical Revelation Explained

by

Patrick J. Sena, C.PP.S.

ALBA · HOUSE   NEW · YORK

SOCIETY OF ST. PAUL, 2187 VICTORY BLVD., STATEN ISLAND, NEW YORK 10314

Library of Congress Cataloging in Publication Data

Sena, Patrick J.
  The Apocalypse: biblical Revelation explained.

  Bibliography: p.
  1. Bible. N.T. Revelation—Commentaries. I. Title.
BS2825.3.S46   1983   228'.07   83-22299
ISBN 0-8189-0454-2

Nihil Obstat:
John J. Jennings
Censor Librorum

Imprimatur:
John L. Cavanaugh
Vicar, Archdiocese of Cincinnati
March 10, 1983

The Nihil Obstat and Imprimatur are
a declaration that a book or pamphlet is considered
to be free from doctrinal or moral error. It is not implied
that those who have granted the Nihil Obstat and
Imprimatur agree with the contents,
opinions or statements expressed.

Designed, printed and bound in the United States of
America by the Fathers and Brothers of the
Society of St. Paul, 2187 Victory Boulevard,
Staten Island, New York 10314, as part of their
communications apostolate.

3 4 5 6 7 8 9 (Current Printing: first digit)

TABLE OF CONTENTS

PREFACE

This work is an attempt to respond to the urgent needs of so many Christians: a simple, understandable presentation of the Book of Revelation. For eleven years I taught an elective course at Mt. St. Mary's Seminary, Cincinnati, Ohio entitled *Understanding the Apocalypse*. It was always well attended. At the same time I had many occasions to teach the Book elsewhere, to give material in workshops, adult education series and retreats throughout the United States and Canada. Always, both great interest and great needs were expressed.

Many people do deserve my thanks. Space, however, limits me to thanking only a few. Special thanks are to be given to Frs. John Dreese, Timothy Schehr, William Kelly, the late Eugene Maly and Dr. Hans Liebenow who during my twelve years at Mt. St. Mary's shared the office of teaching Biblical theology. Many thanks also to the numerous communities of religious women and especially those dedicated to the Blood of Jesus; to the permanent deacons of the Diocese of Amarillo and their Director, Fr. James Gurzynski, who finally convinced me to write this book; to Fr. David Hoying, C.PP.S. who contributed the art work for the cover and to Sr. Elaine Becker, C.PP.S. who typed the final manuscript and offered many helpful suggestions.

It is my hope that this work will prove to be beneficial for Bible study, prayer and a true appreciation for the Book of Revelation.

Patrick J. Sena, C.PP.S.
February 4, 1983
Feast of Blessed Maria de Mattias

HOW TO USE THIS BOOK

This book is divided into three main parts. Part I contains essays from A through W on various necessary topics which need explanation in order to better understand Revelation. Part II contains the actual running commentary on Revelation, divided into twenty-two chapters following the chapters of the Book. Part III contains two appendices treating resources and a teaching methodology. One can begin reading this book by either looking at the essays or using the commentary. In the commentary, the reader will sometimes find a capital letter in parentheses, e.g. (G) or (M) or (U), indicating that there is a complementary treatment to be found in Part I. In the essays there will be mention of other essays which have some bearing upon the one which is currently being read. These, too, will be indicated by (G) or (M) or (U) or any of the other appropriate letters. The book was arranged in this way so as to eliminate an excessive cluttering of the running commentary by taking the reader too far afield with certain background or extended material. It is hoped that this will prove beneficial to the reader in his/her study of Revelation.

PART I

ESSAYS

CONTENTS

A

HISTORICAL BACKGROUND

The author of Revelation is writing to the Christians of Asia Minor, modern day Turkey, to give them hope in the face of persecution. The Emperor Nero had unleashed the first full blown persecution of Christians during his reign (54-68 A.D.). The Roman historian Suetonius recounts the legend that Nero was to come back to life, *Nero redivivus* (G). The Book of Revelation understands that the Emperor Domitian (81-96 A.D.) is in fact the reincarnation of Nero and is now persecuting the Christians of Asia Minor. Suetonius also tells us that during Domitian's reign there was a violent persecution of the Jews and those who lived like Jews (Christians) because they would not pay the exorbitant taxes leveled upon them nor would they acclaim the Emperor as Lord. The persecution and the time of the writing of our work occurred in the mid-90's A.D.

There are countless allusions to these events in our work: *I know where you dwell, where Satan's throne is . . .* (2:13); *Then they were each given a white robe and told to rest a little longer, until the number of their fellow servants and their brethren should be complete, who were to be killed as they themselves had been* (6:11); *These are they who have come out of the great tribulation; they have washed their robes and made them white in the blood of the Lamb* (7:14); *. . . no one can buy or sell unless he has the mark, that is, the name of the beast or the number of its name* (13:16-17).

It should be noted that *the great harlot who is seated upon many waters* (17:1) is the corrupt pagan state of the Roman Empire. The Empire is being depicted in terms of a famous harlot, the wife of Emperor Claudius (41-54 A.D.), whose name was Valeria Messalina. She was so notorious and such a profligate that Claudius had to put her to death. Over one hundred years after her death, her harlotry was recorded by the Roman historian Tacitus and by the Roman satirist Juvenal. In the eyes of Christians, she became an apt symbol of the entire Roman Empire.

B

OVERALL PLAN OF THE BOOK OF REVELATION

Revelation is divided into four basic sections. In each section there is a vision which sets the tone for the remainder of that division.

Part One is found in cc. 1-3. There is an introduction in 1:1-7 followed by the inaugural vision of 1:8-20; cc. 2-3 treat of the seven letters to the seven churches: Ephesus 2:1-7; Smyrna 2:8-11; Pergamum 2:12-17; Thyatira 2:18-29; Sardis 3:1-6; Philadelphia 3:7-13; Laodicea 3:14-22. Because of the prominence of the seven letters, this section is often called "the Seven Letters to the Seven Churches."

Part Two is found in cc. 4-11. There is an inaugural vision in cc. 4-5; the opening of the seven seals in cc. 6-8:1; the sounding of the seven trumpets in cc. 8:2-11:20. This has sometimes been called "the Apocalypse for the Jews," especially since it ends with the ark of the covenant being made visible for all to see and thus approach God (11:19). God's message is no longer directed to one nation, but to all nations.

Part Three is found in cc. 12-20. There is again an inaugural vision in c. 12 which begins the seven signs, *portents* (12:1,3; 13:13,14; 15:1; 16:14; 19:20). This section is often called "the Apocalypse for the Gentiles," especially since it ends with Christ being proclaimed *King of kings and Lord of lords* (19:16) over all the peoples of the world.

Part Four is found in cc. 21-22. There is once more an inaugural vision of the new heaven and the new earth and the new Jerusalem (21:1-8); followed by a description of the new Jerusalem (21:9-22:5); a conclusion of authentication, warning and hope (22:6-21). Because of the prominence of the new Jerusalem, this section often goes by the name of "the New Jerusalem."

C

THE APOCALYPTIC LITERARY FORM

Apocalyptic writing is precisely what the words imply, a kind of writing. Just as there exists historical writing, poetic writing, letter writing and novel writing, there exists apocalyptic writing.

The age of apocalyptic writing covers approximately four hundred years, 200 B.C. to 200 A.D. In the Bible we have two great works written in this apocalyptic style, Revelation and Daniel. Outside the Bible there are many other extant apocalyptic works, e.g., 1 Enoch, 4 Ezra and 2 Baruch. Apocalyptic as a type of writing flourished during periods of upheaval when the Jews or the Christians were suffering for their faith. Daniel was written during the persecution of the Syrian ruler Antiochus IV Epiphanes a. 165 B.C. Revelation was written during the persecution of the Roman Emperor Domitian in the mid-90's A.D. Both works had as their object to impress upon the faithful Jews (Daniel) and the faithful Christians (Revelation) that the Lord would champion his people in the face of the persecution, that the people of God would be victorious in the long run. Therefore, they have every reason for hope. Their enemies will be punished by God (N).

In order to not draw too much attention to themselves, the writers of these works usually used a pseudonym, i.e., did not use their real names. They also used the system of *gematria*, i.e., numbers which signified letters in order to confound the persecutor (F). The people for whom the works were first written understood the meaning because the works were written for people of the same culture and background as the writer.

In order to express hope, these sacred writers focused upon the glory of those who had already triumphed. As those who had gone on before had triumphed, so those who were suffering would also triumph (6:9-11). These people were not looking to some far distant future when God or Jesus would come to champion them; rather, they were looking for a champion in the immediate turmoil of the present moment. Thus they understood that the joy of heaven, which existed for their companions who had been slain, was in fact entering into the present moment upon earth and transforming the pain and persecution into a joyful endurance. Heaven was understood to be breaking into the present. To express the joys of heaven, they heaped up images and colors and movement and song and extraordinary building materials (viz. c. 5 and c. 21).

Apocalyptic literature was a vital part of the literary movement in the ancient Near East. The Book of Revelation is no exception. It should be noted that the Greek word *apocalypsis* and the Latin translation of it, *revelatio*, signify the same reality. The two English words *Apocalypse* and *Revelation* mean exactly the same thing: that which is hidden has been made known.

D

INTERPRETING THE APOCALYPSE

The Apocalypse is not prophecy, as prophecy is so often misunderstood, i.e., a foretelling of some future event (L). It should be noted that prophets were not primarily dealing with the future; rather, they were dealing with the people of their time who had need of repentance. They spoke in God's behalf, calling the faithless to repent and to return to God.

The Apocalypse is written in the apocalyptic literary style (C) and should not be understood as a puzzle which has remained hidden for two thousand years until someone in modern times found a key to understand the Book. Such an approach denies the fact that all Scripture has to have meaning for the people of every age. Such an approach calls into question the goodness of God, who would have revealed a Book of the Bible and then not let anyone understand the true meaning of it until our present age. What kind of God would he be if he had prevented nineteen centuries of Christians from knowing the meaning of Revelation?

Throughout history there have been four basic approaches to understanding the Apocalypse. The first is that the Book treats of the end times and the final days; the second, that the Book treats of a projection of all history of every age leading to the final day of the second coming; the third, that the Book has universal spiritual principles that have meaning for every age; the fourth, that the Book was written for a specific time and a specific occasion: that of the reign of the Emperor Domitian.

The first view has been addressed above. The second view attempts to make the Book a time chart of history: each chapter referring to a specific era in the church, e.g., c. 16, the Protestant Reformation. The third view says that individually and particularly the Book has little value other than to furnish some general principles applicable for all time. Thus there is no point in dealing with the Book in detail. The fourth view, which we propose, says that the Book had an historical meaning when it was written for a specific readership in mind, and that it also has meaning for us today. Much is as relevant for the Christian of every age as was relevant for the first century Christians.

It should be noted that throughout the NT the various sacred authors insist on the fact that Jesus has fulfilled the OT longings, aspirations and prophecies. *The time is fulfilled, and the kingdom of God is at hand; repent, and believe in the gospel* (Mk 1:15). *All this took place to fulfill what the Lord had spoken by the prophet* (Mt 1:22) . . . *but this is what was spoken by the prophet Joel* (Ac 2:16). One author says that with Jesus the final days have begun (Heb 1:2). There is no indication that any NT author thought that the OT prophecies had not been fulfilled in the person of Jesus Christ and his Church. There is one approach of interpreting Revelation which aligns itself with the first view and insists that Christ and the Church never fulfilled the OT prophecies. This interpretation goes by the name of dispensationalism (E). Such an interpretation is to be rejected.

In many ways the Apocalypse is for every age, since it contains enduring themes that apply to every age: hope and steadfastness in the face of evil; raw political, economic or social power as adversaries against Christ and his followers; false religion as undermining the truth. These enduring themes, however, have to be understood against the background of the time when the Book was written.

E

DISPENSATIONALISM

Dispensationalism is a system for interpreting the Bible. Its founder is John Nelson Darby (1800-1882) who had been ordained for the Church of Ireland in 1825; but becoming dissatisfied, he left it to organize the Plymouth Brethren movement in England. A fundamental tenet of dispensationalism is that God has dealt with his people in seven different dispensations or eras, beginning with the first human beings. A list of the seven dispensations is as follows:

1. Innocence -   Adam and Eve
2. Conscience -   Post-Paradise human beings
3. Human government -   Human beings subjected to their
                        fellows
4. Promise -   Abraham and the Patriarchs
5. Law -   The Mosaic covenant and Israel
6. Church -   The post-resurrection time until now
7. Kingdom -   The millennium, the reign of 1000
                        years when the OT promises will be
                        fulfilled.

The Book of Revelation plays an important part in dispensationalist theology. Dispensationalists look very literally at c. 20 and are premillenarians (J). They believe that there is a sharp cleavage between Judaism and Christianity, and that the Church will be raptured (K) before the inauguration of the millennium (J). All of the OT prophecies must be literally fulfilled. Another tenet is that neither Christ nor his Church has fulfilled these prophecies. They especially long for the prophecies of doom upon Israel to be fulfilled. They also see every single verse of Revelation as necessarily being fulfilled when the Church is raptured so that the millennium can begin. This dispensationalist theology and methodology is popularized in *The New Scofield Reference Bible* and by such authors as Hal Lindsey and Salem Kirban and many TV evangelists and personalities. It should also be noted that the Moody Bible Institute is dispensationalist; so is the exegetical magazine *Bibilotheca Sacra*.

The concept of the various dispensations was unknown until the time of John Darby. It runs contrary to the whole history of Biblical interpretation. If there was merit to it, we must ask ourselves once again: why would the good Lord hide the meaning of the Scriptures until the time of John Darby, thus letting millions of Christians remain in ignorance about the central meanings of Christianity? The approach of the dispensationalists is that the Bible is a puzzle book and that all prophecies must be fulfilled in Palestine. It should be noted that this is why so many TV personalities seem to be overjoyed with the present State of Israel—not because the Jewish people once again have a homeland, but because the final days can begin and punishment can be meted out on the unfaithful in Palestine. Mainstream Christianity has rejected the system of dispensationalism.

F

NUMBERS: THEIR SIGNIFICANCE

Among the ancients, numbers held a very important place. Before the invention of the Arabic numerals, letters were used for numbers (V). In the Book of Revelation some numbers occur over and over again. The following is an explanation of the numbers and their significance.

1. 7 was considered to be a perfect number by the ancients. It expressed a totality—so that instead of imagining perfection or every conceivable thing, the ancients would use a 7 to express that meaning. As a number, 7 is explicitly used 43 times in our work. But there are hidden uses of the number 7 as well: e.g., seven references to war (6:4; 9:13-21; 14:19-20; 17:16; 19:17-21; 20:7,9), seven beatitudes (1:3; 14:13; 16:15; 19:9; 20:6; 22:7; 22:14), seven attributes of the Lamb (5:12), seven blessings in heaven (7:15-17).

2. *3* shares in the perfection of 7 and is used explicitly 31 times. At the same time there are clusters of threes which are employed: e.g., the triple *woe* (8:13), the triple *holy* (4:8).

3. *4* shares in the perfection of 7 also and is used explicitly 29 times. It, too, is used in clusters of fours: e.g., four attributes of the Lamb (5:13), four angels in c. 14 (vv. 6, 8, 9, 17).

4. *12*, being a multiple of 3 × 4, also shares in the perfection of 7. It is used 22 times and is also found in conjunction with 1000 (e.g., 7:5-8).

5. *1000* and all numbers with zeroes indicate an unlimited number. Thus, 12,000 signifies a perfect unlimited number; the same can be said for 144,000 (7:4). 1000 is used explicitly 27 times in our work. For a longer discussion of the 1000 year reign cf. (J).

6. *666* is used but one time. For a longer discussion cf. (G).

7. *1260* (11:3) and *42* (11:2) and *3½* (11:9) refer to the same reality. This is the time indicated in Dn 7:25; 12:7 as the period of tribulation. It was the time of the Maccabean revolt (June, 168 B.C.-December, 165 B.C.). The author of Rv has used this time as symbolic of the tribulation time which the early Christians were experiencing during the persecution of the Emperor Domitian.

G

THE BEAST: 13:18

This calls for wisdom: let him who has understanding reckon the number of the beast, for it is a human number, its number is six hundred and sixty-six (13:18).

Because of the statement in the text, the beast is to be identified with some human being whom the people at the time of the writing of the Book would have readily known. It should be noted that some manuscripts read "six hundred and sixteen" and not "six hundred and sixty-six."

Ancient Hebrew/Aramaic did not contain numbers separate from their letters. Like the Romans who used Roman numerals (letters for numbers), so the people of the Bible used their letters as numerals (V).

The first Roman Emperor to persecute the Christians was the Emperor Nero (54-68). Nero is indicated in 13:3: *One of its heads seemed to have a mortal wound, but its mortal wound was healed, and the whole earth followed the beast with wonder* (A). In the Hebrew/Aramaic alphabet the expression "Nero Caesar" in Hebrew would be written in transliteration as follows:

N-50   R-200   W-6   N-50   Q-100   S-60   R-200

Neron   Caesar

In Hebrew and Greek, "Nero" is spelled "Neron" with a final "n." This is not the case in Latin. It is easily seen that someone transliterating from Latin and not realizing that the Hebrew rendition of the Emperor's name contained a final "n," would have omitted the final "n." N is the number 50. For this reason some manuscripts read "six hundred and sixteen" instead of "six hundred and sixty-six." The ancients readily understood that our author was indicating Nero Caesar with the number "six hundred and sixty-six."

H

HYMNS OF THE APOCALYPSE

There are numerous hymns or songs in Revelation. They are to be found generally in the poetic passages of the Book. For the most part they are songs of praise directed to God or the Lamb-Christ: 4:8; 4:11; 5:9-14; 6:10; 7:10; 7:12; 11:15-18; 12:10-12; 15:3-4;

19:1-4; 19:6-7. As hymns they enhance the liturgy of heaven (O). They do point out the liturgical character of the work and the centrality of God and Jesus in the lives of all the pilgrims as they wend their way to the heavenly home. Many songs used in churches today have been inspired by the Book of Revelation: e.g., *Holy, holy, holy* (4:8); *Crown Him With Many Crowns* (19:12); *Blessing and Honor* (5:12); Handel's *Hallelujah Chorus* (11:15; 19:6; 19:16).

Where God and the Lamb are, there is such joy that no one present can really stop singing. By reading and praying these hymns, the Christian can readily discern that the vocation proper to each one is . . . *a sacrifice of praise to God, that is, the fruit of lips that acknowledge his name* (Heb 13:15).

I

USE OF THE OLD TESTAMENT

Revelation is composed of 404 verses, and in at least three-fourths of them there is some allusion to the OT. The OT is never quoted directly but it is the background out of which the author writes and explains his understanding of the Lamb-Christ. The author uses the imagery of the OT and transforms it into a magnificent mosaic to depict the hope-filled consciousness of humanity (P). The Books of the OT which are most frequently used as references are: Exodus, Ezekiel, Zechariah, Daniel, Genesis, Deuteronomy, Numbers and the Psalms.

Any reference Bible will have the appropriate background OT texts listed in the footnotes.

The author is at pains to point out that the Lamb's victory has fulfilled every longing and aspiration of the OT. He reminds us that we are an Exodus people, for we are a journeying people on our way to our permanent home in which every tear will be wiped away

(21:4). Our author would not be a fundamentalist as regards his use of the OT, for he often conflates two different texts to form the background of his text (e.g., 6:1-8 is based on Zc 1:7-17 mixed with Zc 6:1-8). Yet it is on the basis of the OT that he knows that Christ has fulfilled the Father's plan.

J

THE MILLENNIUM: THE 1000 YEAR'S REIGN

The millennium, or the 1000 year reign of Christ upon the earth, has as its focal point the reference made in Rv 20:4-6. The reader's attention is called to the use of numbers (F) in ancient times. The content of the aforementioned vv. has as its focus the fact that even now the Christians who do in fact lead the victorious life are reigning with Christ, *King of kings and Lord of lords* (19:16). The Christian has already *come to Mount Zion and to the city of the living God, the heavenly Jerusalem, and to innumerable angels in festal gathering, and to the assembly of the first-born who are enrolled in heaven, and to a judge who is God of all, and to the spirits of just men made perfect, and to Jesus, the mediator of a new covenant, and to the sprinkled blood that speaks more graciously than the blood of Abel* (Heb 12:22-24). Christ reigns now!

Many fundamentalist Christians are premillennialists; i.e., they look forward to the actual reign of 1000 years during which time they will publicly rule with the Lord. Throughout history individuals have predicted the 1000 year reign as immanent, but it never came in the way in which it was predicted. One must understand the millennium within the context of the persecution of the Christians by the Emperor Domitian. Those Christians who lost their lives have been reigning with Christ in a very special way from heaven from that time until now. 1000 signifies a limitless reign with the Lord. In another sense, all Christians who are living the victorious life of grace are also even now reigning with the Lord.

Dispensationalism (E) is above all premillenarian. It looks forward to an actual 1000 year reign, no more and no less. This is not in accord with the mainstream of Christian thought.

K

THE RAPTURE

In the Greek Bible there is nowhere mentioned any such thing as a rapture. The term, however, is common in certain fundamentalist circles. In spiritual theology the term is used of the ecstatic trances of the great mystics such as St. Teresa of Avila.

It would seem that the term itself owes its origin to the Latin Vulgate, the translation of the Bible made by St. Jerome a. 400 A.D. In Latin the word *rapio* means "to seize or snatch." It is found in 2 Cor 12:4 and in 1 Th 4:17. In the first citation it refers to Paul's mystical experience; in the second citation it refers to the Second Coming of the Lord, where both the context and the language employed in the Greek original tell us that the Lord will come as a king. Such language as found in 1 Th 4:14-17 is typical of the language used to describe the arrival of the Emperor or some far-eastern potentate. It is typical of apocalyptic language used to describe a very wondrous event (C).

Dispensationalists and other fundamentalist Christians believe that the rapture will occur for the Church during the time of the great battle when Satan will be loosed (20:7). The Church will be taken out of this world and the OT prophecies leveled against Israel will be fulfilled (E).

There does not appear to be any solid foundation in the Bible for holding the teaching about the rapture. As a special teaching associated with the end times, it became popular only in the nineteenth century.

L

PROPHECY IN REVELATION

The word properly translated "prophet" in the OT is *nabi*, which means "one who announces God's plan" or, used in the passive, "one who is called by God." The basic connotation is not about the future plan which might not affect the lives of the faithful now, but rather about God's plan for those to whom the prophet gives his message.

In our book the word *prophet* is found eight times: 10:7; 11:10; 11:18; 16:6; 18:20, 24; 22:6,9). The message given by our author is one of hope to a suffering and persecuted Christian community during the reign of Domitian. It is the same message of hope which pertains to every generation of Christians, for in every generation there has always been some form of suffering and persecution (P).

The author is not speaking about the end of time, which would have little relevancy to his readers. The words which he uttered had meaning for the first generation of Christians, for as he says, *the time is near* (1:3) for the words to come true.

We should not be misled by fundamentalist or dispensationalist teaching in this matter. Paul says that *he who prophesies speaks to men for their upbuilding and encouragement and consolation* (1 Cor 14:3). Our author, as prophet, has written to give encouragement, strength and consolation to the faithful, suffering Christian. He has not written to foretell doom and destruction upon the faithless as such (N), but only insofar as they have not ceased to harm God's chosen ones.

M

THE LETTERS

In cc. 2-3 we find the seven letters to the seven churches in Asia Minor: Ephesus (2:1-7); Smyrna (2:8-11); Pergamum (2:12-17);

Thyatira (2:18-29); Sardis (3:1-6); Philadelphia (3:7-13); and La-odicea (3:14-22). They are all written in a typical letter style of writing. Thus, the Book of Revelation is not only an apocalyptic writing (C); it also contains the epistolary style of writing.

All seven of our letters have the same components, so that if we were to put them side by side this is what we would find: 1) a salutation which is identical for all seven cities except for the name of the city; 2) the identification of Christ, which is the same for all seven insofar as they begin with *The words of*; 3) compliments which are bestowed upon five of the churches, there being no word of praise for Sardis or Laodicea; 4) rebukes which are bestowed upon five of the churches, there being no reprimand for Smyrna or Philadelphia; 5) an exhortation to either repent or remain faithful as the case may be, always ending with the phrase: *He who has an ear let him hear what the Spirit says to the churches*; 6) a promise in every case *for he who conquers*.

The identification of Christ often refers back to the inaugural vision in 1:12-20.

The use of seven (F) as the complete number is representative of the fact that the author wanted to speak about various problems in the whole Church. He knew his geography well, because the Romans had built a circular road in Asia Minor and if one were to begin a journey at Ephesus on that road and not leave the road, he would pass through the remaining six churches. After visiting Laodicea, the next church on the journey would once again be Ephesus. He knew these churches very well, since much of the history or the social status or the economy of these cities is mentioned in his description of them.

N

THE CATASTROPHES

The various catastrophic events portrayed in Revelation are directed not to those who bear the Lamb's or his Father's name upon their foreheads (14:1), but rather upon *those who dwell on the earth* (3:10; 6:10; 8:13; 11:10; 13:8,12,14; 17:2,8), those who *are marked on the right hand or forehead* (13:16) with the mark of the beast's name. These individuals are subservient to the beast and are enemies of the Christians (R).

These terrible events are reminiscent of the events which happened during the first Exodus when Moses led the people out of Egypt (cf. Ex 7:20-21; 9:8, 23-27; 10:14,21; 19:16-19). The faithful Christians remain safe from the *wrath of the Lamb* (6:16). This is what c. 7 is all about.

These events form part of the apocalyptic style of writing (C), and should in no way be taken as prophecies (L) about that which is to take place. Above all, the catastrophes—earthquakes, hail, fire, plagues, lightning, the disintegration of the heavens—show that God is in control. He is the provident one and his enemies will be defeated by his creation. They will have no absolute power over his people or his creation, even though at times they may seem to have gained the upper hand.

O

LITURGICAL CHARACTER OF THE BOOK

Together with the Epistle to the Hebrews, this work is one of the two most liturgical of the NT writings. It is a Book of victory, and the reader is transported to the heavenly throne room (cc. 4-5) to get a glimpse of the worship ceremony of praise which is being conducted therein.

For that reason, there are many hymns (H) scattered throughout the Book. For that same reason, the work is filled with prayers (e.g., 1:5b-7; 22:20-21; the seven beatitudes, cf. 1:3).

The book reminds us that worship entails not merely the use of the head, i.e., the intellectual aspect of humanity, but also the total use of the body-person. For this reason, heaven is said to be a place of singing (19:6), a place of movement (4:10), a place of color (21:19f), a place of musical instruments (5:8), a place where there is the odor of incense (5:8), a place of listening (5:11). The entire activity of the book occurs on the *Lord's day* (1:10).

We Christians are being told that when we worship here below, we are already being joined to our associates who are worshipping now in God's presence. Heaven is breaking into our present existence (C). There is a communion of saints: we are united to those who have gone before us and are resting in God's presence (6:9-11). The Christians who were being persecuted by Domitian understood this; we should understand it as well.

P

HOPE-FILLED VICTORY

Throughout history, Revelation has enjoyed special attention during difficult times. There is a great deal of devotional literature which has sprung forth from the Nazi prison camps of World War II. During times of stress, Christians have readily turned to Revelation for hope and consolation.

Revelation is about the last pilgrimage which each Christian must make: a pilgrimage from this world to the next; a pilgrimage during which we get a glimpse into that which will come; a pilgrimage which is guided by the Lord who is acting even now in our lives.

The image of the Lamb (Q) has become the apt image of victory and hope. We know that he is alive even though he once died (5:6). Where he now is perfectly acclaimed as *King of kings and Lord of lords* (19:16), we hope to one day be. Indeed, the Lamb-Jesus has become our shepherd (7:17) so that no danger can beset us. Even should we be killed and left to lie in the streets while our enemies rejoice (11:9-10), nevertheless, we shall be victorious and rise with

the Lord (11:11). We are immune to the ravages of all the forces of
Satan. They can never permanently harm us.

Q
THE CENTRALITY OF CHRIST

We find various titles or names for Christ throughout the work.
He is called *Jesus Christ* (1:2); *faithful witness, the firstborn of the
dead, and ruler of kings on earth* (1:5); *one like a son of man* (1:13);
the first and the last (1:17); *the Son of God* (2:18); *the holy one, the
true one* (3:7); *the Amen, the faithful and true witness, the beginning of God's creation* (3:14); *the Lion of the tribe of Judah, the
Root of David* (5:5); *a Lamb standing, as though it had been slain*
(5:6) (an image used predominantly from this point on for a total of
28 times); *the bright morning star* (22:16); *the Alpha and Omega*
(22:13).

Christ as Lamb is the most common designation for Jesus
beginning with c. 5 and continuing down to c. 22. The OT background to the Lamb imagery is taken from Is 53:7 which speaks of
the Servant of God who is led like a lamb to the slaughter, and Ex
12:21 which recounts the killing of the paschal lamb.

Christ is the victorious Lamb, since he stands with the marks of
his wounds upon his body (5:6). There is hardly any chapter that
does not have some reference to Christ as the victorious Lamb. The
author uses a mixed imagery when he says: *For the Lamb in the
midst of the throne will be their shepherd, and he will guide them to
springs of living water; and God will wipe away every tear from
their eyes* (7:17).

R
SATANIC FIGURES

The Book shows a triumvirate of evil: the dragon, the sea beast
and the land beast or false prophet.

The dragon is called the *ancient serpent . . . Devil and Satan, the deceiver of the whole world* (12:9). He is specifically called "dragon" twelve times (12:3,4,7,9,13,16,17; 13:2,4,11; 16:13; 20:2). The title "Devil" is used five times (2:10; 12:9,12; 20:2,10). As "Satan" he is mentioned eight times (2:9, 13 [twice], 24; 3:9; 12:9; 20:2,7).

The word "beast" occurs thirty times, sometimes referring to the beast from the sea (13:1; 20:10); at other times referring to the false prophet or land beast (13:11) (G).

Evil has its origins with the Devil who transmits it to the pagan state which in turn passes it on to false religion. It is the evil which is at odds with Christianity. It is this evil which has always tried to slay those who believe in Christ, and to make them sway from following the truth.

But throughout it all, *the King of kings and Lord of lords* (U) conquers and casts the dragon, the beast and the false prophet into the bottomless pit (20:10).

S

ARMAGEDDON

And they assembled them at the place which is called in Hebrew Armageddon (16:16).

There is no other mention of a place called Armageddon in the Bible or any other writing of the time or upon any map of the ancient world.

Some manuscripts for 16:16 read *Harmagedon* which would be equivalent to the Hebrew for Mount Megiddo, *Har* meaning "mountain" and *megedon* for Megiddo. The Hebrew rendering of Megiddo in Zc 12:11 is *meggedon*.

Another suggestion is that the phrase stands for *har migdo* in Hebrew which means "his fruitful mountain"—which would then suggest Mount Zion, which is mentioned in 14:1.

However, it would seem that the mountain of Megiddo might be the best explanation. Megiddo was located on a pass between the coastal plains of Palestine and the interior Plain of Esdraelon where numerous battles had taken place. Syria and Egypt would wage their battles here at the half way post between the two countries. King Josiah lost his life there (2 Ch 35:22) and Barak and Sisera also had an encounter there (Jg 5:19).

It would appear that our author is using figurative language in terms of the great battlefield, which was known through the OT chronicling of the people of God, to speak about the final battle when everyone would acclaim Jesus as the *Word of God* (19:13). At that time all of God's enemies will be defeated—not by armaments, but by his Incarnate Word, Jesus.

T

HEADS AND HORNS (17:7)

But the angel said to me, "Why marvel? I will tell you the mystery of the woman, and of the beast with seven heads and ten horns that carries her" (17:7).

The seven heads correspond to the seven Emperors beginning with Nero.

Nero   (54-68)
Galba   (68-69)
Otho   (69)
Vitellius   (69)
Vespasian   (69-79)
Titus   (79-81)
Domitian   (81-96)

The beast that you saw was, and is not, and is to ascend from the bottomless pit and go to perdition (17:8) is a reference to the legend about Nero returning to life and coming back as his successor Domitian, *Nero redivivus* (A).

The ten horns, as the author notes, refer to ten vassal kings (17:12) whose identities have been lost to history.

U

KING OF KINGS AND LORD OF LORDS: 19:16

Ancient Hebrew/Aramaic did not contain numbers separate from their letters. Like the Romans who used Roman numerals (letters in place of separate numbers), so the people of the Bible used their letters as numerals (V). In 19:16 the phrase *King of kings and Lord of lords* has been transmitted in the best Greek lower case manuscripts (minuscules: manuscripts in which no capital letters are found) in upper case letters; i.e., each letter of the word is a capital. This indicates that the phrase is very special. There is only one other example of this in our work and that is to be found in 17:5 where there is a special title: *Babylon the great, mother of harlots and of earth's abominations.* 17:5 refers to the pagan Roman Empire which was persecuting the early Christians.

In the Hebrew/Aramaic alphabet the expression found in 19:16 would be written in transliteration as follows:

M-40 L-30 K-20 M-40 L-30 K-20 Y-10 N-50 M-40 R-200 '-1 M-40 R-200 W-6 N-50

KING	OF KINGS	LORD	OF LORDS
90	150	241	296

Thus, 90 + 150 + 241 + 296 = 777. A triple 7 indicates a perfect number (F). Jesus has the perfect name and it is fitting that he is the one to conquer the devil, the beast and the false prophet (20:10).

V

THE HEBREW ALPHABET: ITS FIXED NUMERICAL SIGNIFICANCE

Biblical Hebrew does not contain any written vowels. The same alphabet with the same numerical equivalents is utilized in Biblical Aramaic. Like the Latins, whose Roman numerals were really letters, so, too, the Hebrews utilized letters to indicate their numerals. The letters always signify the same fixed numbers.

Name	Transliteration into English Characters	Number
Aleph	' (smooth breathing mark)	1
Beth	b	2
Gimel	g	3
Daleth	d	4
He (hay)	h	5
Waw	w	6
Zayin	z	7
Heth (kath)	h	8
Teth	t	9
Yodh	y	10
Kaph	k	20
Lamedh	l	30
Mem	m	40
Nun	n	50
Samekh	s	60

'Ayin	' (rough breathing mark)	70
Pe	p	80
Cadhe (Sadhe)	s	90
Qoph	q	100
Resh	r	200
Sin, Shin	s ś	300
Taw	t	400

W

AUTHOR

A characteristic of apocalyptic writing is not to append the real name of the author to the work (C). It would seem that Revelation is no exception. The author calls himself John (1:9). We have no indication whatsoever that this is John the apostle. To be sure, John was a common enough name in NT times just as it is today, so that he might actually be giving us his real name. The Greek manuscript contains the poorest Greek in the entire NT, which indicates that the author did not use Greek as his principal language—that in fact, it was an acquired language. Both the grammar and syntax are exceedingly poor. In 1:8: *I am the Alpha and the Omega*, in the original would be written as follows: I am the *alpha* and the *o*. That is, he writes out the *alpha*, but leaves the letter *o* instead of writing *omega*. A sure indication of a sloppy writing style.

It really makes no difference who the human author is of any book of the Bible. What does make the difference is the fact that it is God's word for us. Some have said that since the writing of the Apocalypse is so different from the Gospel of John and since we get the impression that the apostles were fishermen and probably had

little education, it just might be that the Apocalypse was written by
the apostle, but the Gospel and Letters by someone else.

PART II

COMMENTARY

CONTENTS

CONTENTS

CHAPTER 1

THE INAUGURAL VISION

1:1-2 Revelation is a translation of the Greek word *apocalypsis* and the Latin *revelatio*. This is the origin of the two titles for this Book: *Revelation* which comes through the Latin translation of the original Greek, or *Apocalypse* which comes directly from the Greek original. Both titles are interchangeable (C). *Must soon take place* relates to the immediate background at the time of writing during the persecution of the Roman Emperor Domitian and to God's vindication of his persecuted people. The role of John (W), whose identity cannot be precisely determined, is to explain the *testimony of Jesus Christ*. The Greek word for *testimony* or *witness* is the English word *martyr*. Jesus, the Savior, who is Christ, the Anointed One/Messiah, is presented to the reader as the first authentic martyr of the new age. These introductory verses are typical of apocalyptic writing (C).

1:3 With this verse we encounter the first of seven beatitudes scattered throughout the work (1:3; 14:13; 16:15; 19:9; 20:6; 22:7; 22:14) (F). The vocabulary of 22:7 is similar to 1:3 and is thus a companion beatitude located at the end of the work. The author wishes to indicate that whoever reads the work and takes it to heart will be blessed indeed. *Prophecy* (L) as such does not concern itself with the future; a prophet is one who speaks in God's name to the people of his own day, making known God's message for them.

1:4-7 A compact unit describing the eternity of God: *is . . .*

was . . . is to come; the fullness of the Spirit: *seven spirits*; and the centrality of *Jesus Christ*. As *faithful witness*, Jesus is the one who laid down his life for us out of *love*. As *firstborn of the dead* he is the one who *has freed us . . . by his blood*. As *ruler of the kings on earth, he has made us a kingdom*. He has fulfilled the OT image as presented in Dn 7:13 by receiving power from his Father seated upon the throne in heaven. Jesus Christ is the true king (not the Roman Emperor); those who refuse to accept him *will wail on account of him*. This is the first of many prayers (O) found in the Apocalypse, thus demonstrating the liturgical character of the work.

1:8 By calling himself the *Alpha*, first letter of the Greek alphabet, and the *Omega* (W), last letter, God is pointing out that he is the sum total of all things. The Catholic Church uses this verse in the blessing of the Easter candle ritual on Holy Saturday.

1:9-11 The human author identifies himself by the name John, and points out his solidarity with the reader who is a *brother* who has suffered in Jesus' name just as the first readers suffered during the persecution of the Emperor. A locality is given: Patmos, a small island off the coast of modern Izmir (Smyrna), Turkey. We are told that all that will take place occurs in a vision (O) on Sunday, the *Lord's day* (v. 9). The seven local churches (M) were to be found in Asia Minor, present day Turkey. They were connected by a circular road which had been built by the Romans. Beginning with the seacoast town of Ephesus, one could traverse through all the cities in the order listed by way of this circular road, and once having gone through Laodicea, the next city along the road would be the city of origin, Ephesus. The geographical indications for these cities have been verified by archeologists.

1:12-16 The vision in which *one like a son of man* (v. 13) predominates owes its artistry to Dn 7:9-14. The Dn imagery is adapted by our author for his own purposes. There is a sevenfold physical description of Jesus who continues to walk in the midst of the churches which he has founded. He is not one who has returned to the Father's home and left us abandoned. Rather, he is one who remains close to his people. He is a providential and loving Savior. He holds the whole church, *seven stars*, in his strong right hand in a protective gesture. He seems to have the whole world in his hands. His only armament is his word which comes forth from his mouth as *a sharp two-edged sword*; no other weapons are necessary (Heb 4:12). The robe and girdle point to a priestly garment worn by one who is a priest; the whiteness of the hair indicates his eternal wisdom; the fiery eyes depict his omniscience: he knows all things; his strong feet point to his steadfastness: he cannot be shaken; his strong voice bespeaks his great power and might. The brightness of his face points to his divinity.

1:17-20   The faithful who read Revelation need not fear (v. 17). The same hand which holds the seven stars (v. 16) now directly comforts John. The Lord touches him and makes three claims: this one like a son of man is identified as divine: *the first and the last*; as Jesus: *died . . . and am alive*; as all powerful over our enemies: *keys of Death and Hades*. John is instructed to write down this message and its significance for the reader who is undergoing persecution. Verse 20 explains a part of the inaugural vision.

CHAPTER 2

THE QUARTET OF CHURCHES: EPHESUS, SMYRNA, PERGAMUM, THYATIRA

2:1 We have a reference back to the vision of 1:12-16 as identifying Christ as the one *who holds the seven stars in his right hand.* Ephesus was a coastal city; Roman roads began and ended there (M). The Temple of Diana (Artemis), located in Ephesus, was one of the wonders of the ancient world. Paul ran into conflict with the tradesmen who made their living from Diana's Temple (Ac 19:23-40). With the destruction of Jerusalem (70 A.D.), Ephesus came to be a leading Christian center. Paul had much respect for the church of Ephesus; he summoned the elders to Miletus where they listened to him as he instructed them. They wept when it was time for Paul to leave, for they knew that it would be their last time to be with him (Ac 20:17-38).

2:2-5 Contained in these verses are the accomplishments of the Ephesians: their ability to discern evil in their midst, and their patient endurance. At the same time, a reprimand is in order. It would seem that apathy had won the day and that their love had grown cold. An imperative is given them: *Remember, Repent,* and *Do.* These are the three aspects of any true conversion experience.

2:6 Nicolaitans are also mentioned in 2:15 in the context of Balaam. The Balaam story is recounted in Nb 22-24. In rabbinic literature, Balaam came to be understood as a symbol of false prophecy and prophets. The Nicolaitans then may have been false prophets or sorcerers.

2:7 This is the common ending for all seven of the letters, along with its specific promise for Ephesus. The conqueror will *eat of the tree of life in the paradise of God*. All of the promises see fulfillment in the latter chapters of the Book. The tree of life is mentioned in 22:2.

2:8 Smyrna was due north of Ephesus and possessed a Temple to Tiberius, where Emperor worship was practiced. The identification of the speaker refers back to 1:12-16.

2:9-10 *Poverty* and *rich* are words very reminiscent of 2 Cor 8:9. After all, the Christian life is to be fashioned after the life of Christ, who became poor that we might become rich. So too, the poverty of the Smyrnians is really wealth. False accusations have been leveled against them by a *synagogue of Satan* (cf. 3:9). True Jews are God's children; therefore, whoever is falsely accusing the Christians of Smyrna cannot be a true Jew. Some authors feel that these false Jews were a certain group who had allowed pagan practices to infiltrate their religion. This is the first mention of the devil in the Book. *Ten days* refers to an undetermined period of time (F). The *crown* is characteristic of the conqueror (4:4; 4:10; 6:2; 9:7; 12:1; 14:14).

2:11 The conqueror will not suffer the *second death*. "Second death" is final condemnation and banishment from God (21:8). It should be noted that no reprimand has been given to the church of Smyrna.

2:12 Pergamum was the most important center of Emperor worship in the eastern Empire, having had a Temple erected to Augustus there in 27 B.C. The bellicose imagery of 1:12-16, *the sharp two-edged sword*, is used to identify the speaker. The Roman Proconsul had his headquarters at Pergamum.

2:13-16 *Satan's throne* refers to the Proconsul's headquarters. *Hold fast my name* indicates that the Christians are suffering precisely because they will not offer worship to the Emperor as a divine being. They worship only the name of Jesus. Nothing is known of the man Antipas other than the fact that he was a faithful witness (1:5) who gave his life for the Lord. They are reprimanded at length because of the Nicolaitans and Balaam (2:6). According to Ac 15:20, Gentile converts were to abstain from eating food sacrificed to idols and from the practice of immorality. It is precisely these things which the Pergamum church seems to be practicing.

2:17 This verse speaks of *hidden manna* and a *new name*. The conqueror does not eat idolatrous food (v. 14), but hidden manna (the heavenly food of Heb 9:4). Moses had ordered some manna to be stored in the Ark of the Covenant (Ex 16:32-34). Jeremiah hid the Ark with its manna, according to 2 M 2:4-8. When God would gather his people together, then he would reveal the Ark and its contents(2 M 2:7). Thus, *hidden manna* is another symbol of the promise of paradise. *New name* is that which is written on the foreheads of God's servants who enter into the heavenly city (22:4). *White stone* is reminiscent of the free meal tickets which ancient athletes received.

2:18 Thyatira was a garrison city on the eastern frontier of the Roman province of Asia. Its troops kept the circular road clear and in the hands of the Romans between the cities of Pergamum and Sardis. This is the only time in the book that the expression *Son of God* (Q) is used; he is the speaker who is distinguished by his piercing eyes and the firm setting of his feet.

2:19-23 The local church was unusually tolerant of this woman *Jezebel* in their midst. The main problem with the church at Thyatira was apathy born of complacency. This situation finds a quasi-parallel in 1 Cor 5:1-8. The story of the historical Jezebel is recounted in 1K cc. 16, 18, 19, 21; 2K c. 9. She was the wife of King Ahab, and was the source of untold problems and persecution for the prophet Elijah. The Jezebel of our verse seems to be leading the local people astray. The same false practices are mentioned in v. 20 as for the church in Pergamum (v. 14). The woman had been given the opportunity for repentance, but she had not done so (v. 21); thus, her guilt is grave indeed.

2:24-28 Verse 27 is based upon the messianic Psalm 2:8-9. It is Jesus who is called the morning star in 22:16. For the one who conquers, the promise is that he will possess the light of the dawn of a new day, the bright morning star (v. 28).

CHAPTER 3

THE TRIO OF CHURCHES:
SARDIS, PHILADELPHIA, LAODICEA

3:1 Sardis had been the capital of ancient Lydia (M). It was known for its industry of dyeing wool. Its citadel was located on Mt. Tmolus, which made it almost enemy-proof. Nevertheless, the city had fallen twice to its enemies because of a lack of vigilance.

3:2-3 A very severe rebuke is given to Sardis, but no specific sins or failings are mentioned. It would appear that apathy had once again raised its head in the midst of the Lord's church. Four commands are given: *Awake, Strengthen, Remember, Repent.* As the city had fallen in the past because of a lack of vigilance, so now the citizens are reminded to be watchful or else the Lord may *come like a thief.*

3:4-6 *To walk with Christ in white* is seen as a double reward for the conqueror. The *book of life* assures one of salvation (20:15). Judgment comes about according to *what was written in the books, by what they (the dead) had done* (20:12).

3:7 Philadelphia was a rich commercial center whose economy was supported by the rich volcanic soil suitable for grape growing. The city had been damaged in an earthquake in 17 A.D. *Philadelphia* is a Greek word meaning *brotherly love.* The reference to *key* refers back to 1:18. The other words of the description, *holy* and *true*, are predicated of God in 6:10. Philadelphia was located on the border with Phrygia: the symbolism of the open door may indicate the missionary opportunities for the Philadelphian Christians.

3:8-11 In 3:9 is reiterated what was said of Smyrna in 2:9. The expression*those who dwell on the earth* (v. 10) is also found in 6:10; 8:13; 11:10; 13:8, 12, 14; 17:2, 8. It signifies all those who are opposed to following the Lamb. The Christian is one who has been called to live in heaven and make his permanent dwelling place there. The persecutors are those who dwell on the earth. All the catastrophes of the book are directed to those who dwell on the earth (N).

3:12-13 No reprimand is given to Philadelphia. These verses are very tender ones. There is a sevenfold use of the first person singular pronoun/adjective *I/my*. There is also a threefold combination of names: *the name of my God*; *the name of the city of my God*; *and my own new name*. It would seem that there was the practice in the city of Philadelphia of inscribing the names of noteworthy citizens on the pillars of the many temples. The faithful Christian will belong to the Father, be protected by Christ, and have a permanent dwelling place in the New Jerusalem (21:2). To know someone's name is to have a special relationship with that individual; the Christian will be put into a very close relationship with the Father, Christ, and the heavenly city and its inhabitants.

3:14 Laodicea was located ten miles to the west of Colossae and six miles south of Hierapolis. The city was known for its raven-black wool and its famous eye ointment. Paul's coworker, Epaphras, worked hard for the establishment of the church at Laodicea (Col 4:12-13).

3:15-19 Herein is delivered the most severe rebuke of all the letters. The Laodiceans are accused of being lukewarm, proud and blind. They felt themselves to be self-sufficient. They refused to take a stand for Christ. Verses 16 and 19 are two of the best known of the entire book: the first because it is the harshest of condemnations; the second because it speaks of chastisement because of love.

The raven wool and eye salve of the Laodiceans is not where their wealth ought to lie.

3:20-22 Table fellowship is the promise given to the Laodiceans. The Lord is waiting to enter and dine with them if they will but let him. He invites them to the wedding supper of the Lamb (19:9). Those who are faithful in following Christ are given the promise of being enthroned with him.

CHAPTER 4

IN PRAISE OF GOD OUR CREATOR

4.1-2 So far the activity of the Book has taken place on earth. Christ has been present to comfort, reprimand and hold out rewards to the seven churches. The focus now shifts to heaven and the activity therein. It is well to note that in Bible times the composition of the universe was considered in a very basic, uncomplicated way: the earth was a flat surface, a vault above it was called heaven and there was an underworld below the earth. The *open door* has OT precedents: Ezk 1:1 sees the heavens rolled back so that Ezekiel can look into them. In the apocalyptic non-canonical book 1 Enoch 14:15, gates are seen in heaven and Enoch enters into heaven through those various gates. John had previously seen the one who spoke to him (1:12-16); now he only hears the voice. The literary character of the work now presents the author as having some type of mystical experience perhaps somewhat similar to Paul's in 2 Cor 12:1-4. *Throne* is a word which is used in all of the various settings of the book, except c. 15, to depict God as the enthroned one who rules over all things. Song, colors, movement, awe abound in the two cc. 4-5 which treat of the same heavenly scene (O).

4:3-6 The appearance of the *one seated on the throne* is not described in any ordinary fashion. Rather, he has the appearance of precious stones. In fact, the enthroned one is described in terms of those things which are about him. When Moses had received the Law, we are told that there was lightning, thunder, clouds, a trumpet blast and a trembling people (Ex 19:16). The *twenty-four elders* have been variously interpreted. However, based upon the understanding of the unity of the work, it is best to view them as representing the twelve tribes of Israel and the twelve apostles of the Lamb (21:12-14). Thus, they represent the whole of the people of God: OT and NT. They are victorious, for they are clothed in white (3:5) and have received a crown (2:10). The seven torches of fire seem to represent the same reality as the seven golden lampstands (1:12): the Church on earth is represented even in the heavenly courtroom by the guiding spirit. *A sea of glass like crystal* is a concrete expression of the kingly rule of God. Emperors and kings had a throne room, and before their thrones there was a stone or marble pavement. In a day when glass was a most precious commodity, our author has seen God's throne room as far superior to any earthly king's. *The four living creatures* have been adapted from Ezk 1:4-14 and Is 6:2. Each of Ezekiel's creatures had four different faces and the multitude of eyes were arranged on wheels. The feature of the six wings comes from Isaiah. These creatures with so many eyes can perceive everything; nothing escapes their vision.

4:7-8 These four creatures do not represent the four evangelists. As was mentioned, the description is a composite and adaptation by our author of Ezk and Is. The use of the number 4 probably comes from the four points of the compass. By use of the imagery of a man, a wild animal, a domestic animal and a bird we see that God has dominion over all life forms, and all life forms praise him. Their function is precisely to praise God at all times. The hymn of 4:8 has drawn its inspiration from Is 6:3. The triple use of the term *holy* emphasizes God's complete otherness. God is kingly; he is not like human beings; he is *Almighty*. Absolute holiness belongs only to God who is seated upon his throne. The phrase, *who was and is and is to come* emphasizes God's eternity.

4:9-11 The function of the four living creatures is to give directions to all those who are involved in the public worship of heaven.

They act as masters of ceremonies and are mentioned fourteen times in the Book. Their purpose is to *give glory, honor and thanks.* The twenty-four elders are mentioned twelve times in the work. They are to worship the one seated on the throne; to do so they take off their crowns of glory to acknowledge his absolute majesty. In worshipping God they render to him that gift which he has given them, the crown of glory. Verse 11 is a new song which the elders sing, giving a threefold acclamation of the Lord God's worthiness: *glory, honor and power* belong to him because he is the creator of all things and because they continue to exist because of him.

CHAPTER 5

IN PRAISE OF CHRIST,
THE REDEEMING LAMB

5:1-2 The one seated upon the throne had been described in terms of light and of color (4:3). Now a right hand comes forth from that auroral image; it contains a seven-sealed scroll. Ezk 2:9-10 contains a similar type of scroll with a message for the prophet. It is most difficult to picture the scroll of c. 5; as in Ezk so in this scroll, God's message is contained for his people. The heavenly angel endeavors to find someone who can unravel the scroll and thus explain God's message contained in it.

5:3-4 In 4:11 God himself had been acclaimed as the worthy one. John weeps because no one at all has been found sufficiently worthy to open and explain the scroll. The entire book is filled with drama. John weeps, thus involving the reader in his plight.

5:5-7 Immediately one of the elders steps up to John, who is standing in the doorway of heaven (4:1), and tells him not to cry for someone has been found to explain the scroll. That someone (Q) is the *Lion of the tribe of Judah, the Root of David* (v. 5). Gn 49:9 speaks of Judah as *a lion's whelp*. This statement was later used by the rabbis to point out Messianic fulfillment. Lions used to be found in great numbers along the Ghor Valley of the Jordan river. *Root of David* finds its origin in the expression in Is 11:10, *root of Jesse* (David's father), which was later used as a Messianic prophecy. John does not see a Lion, but what he sees in the very midst of the heavenly throne room is a *Lamb standing as though it had been slain*. It is the Passover lamb, Jesus Christ who has conquered and stands erect, having gloriously arisen and ascended to the heavenly Father. The marks of his slaying, the wounds, are evident. But he is glorious. He has the fullness of power, *seven horns;* the fullness of knowledge, *seven eyes* (F). He takes the scroll, which is understood to be God's message as revealed in the OT. The victorious Lamb is the fulfillment of that message: only he can interpret it. Thus, the seven-sealed scroll should be understood as the content of the OT. Because of Jesus Christ, the victorious Lamb, God's plan of creation has been fulfilled in his redeeming plan involving the Incarnate Son.

5:8-14 The *new song* (v. 9) is now sung (H). The Lamb is standing in the midst of all the other inhabitants of heaven: the twenty-four elders, the four living creatures, God upon his throne, the angels of heaven and all creation. *Harp* and *incense* point out the liturgical character of the heavenly worship. The whole person is involved in worship: voice, smell, sight, sound, movement. All in heaven sing a song in praise of redemption, in praise of the *blood* (v. 8). The blood of Jesus fulfills the OT understanding that blood is the bearer of life itself (Gn 9:4; Lv 17:11). The song is one of thanksgiving for life; Domitian and his persecutors may have taken the earthly lives of faithful Christians, but they have gained eternal life because of the Lamb's lifeblood. All peoples have been called into the kingdom of Jesus (v. 10); all are called to rule because they share God's power (3:21) in having overcome the oppression by remaining faithful to Jesus. The Lamb who had died and come to life again (2:8), the Son of God (2:18), has been found worthy. Verse 12 appoints seven adjectives to describe the Lamb; a perfect acclamation of his worthiness. Verse 13 appoints four adjectives for the Lamb and the one upon the throne; a universal acclamation for them. Verse 14 resounds with the great *Amen* of the heavenly hosts. It should be noted that this new song in heaven (v. 9) begins its crescendo with the twenty-four elders and the four living creatures (v. 8) who are very close to the Lamb and to God. It continues with the angels who hover about the heavenly throne, numbering into the multiples of thousands (v. 11); they are further away. Then every creaturegets involved in this song *in heaven and on earth and under the earth and in the sea*. This is all followed by the great Amen. The song begun in heaven has gone forth to all the universe. In c. 19 the shock waves of great rejoicing begin first with the great multitude of heaven (19:1), then the twenty-four elders and the four living creatures (19:5). Effectively what we have between c. 5 and c. 19 is an accordion effect: the song has gone forth into the universe in c. 5 and has returned to its origin, heaven itself, in c. 19.

The scene which we have just witnessed in cc. 4-5 can be visualized if one imagines that he or she is standing in the doorway of some great cathedral during a solemn celebration at which the local bishop is present. One would see the bishop seated upon his throne, his attendant concelebrating priests, his deacons and minor ministers about the altar which would be central in the sanctuary. In the nave of the church, the faithful would be gathered and choirs would be singing accompanied by musical instruments. The whole church would be filled with the sweet-smelling odor of incense.

Our author is telling us that heaven will be the greatest celebration (O) which can be imagined. It will be far greater than anything on earth. The citizens of earth are joined to their heavenly counterpart whenever they enter into communal worship. All Christian worship is praise, *the fruit of lips that acknowledge his name* (Heb 13:15).

CHAPTER 6

THE OPENING OF THE FIRST SIX SEALS

6:1-2 The word *come* contains within it a certain urgency. These things of which the author speaks in his apocalyptic vision are to happen in the near future. The background from which the four horsemen come is a compilation from Zc 1:7-17 and 6:1-8. By combining them, John has come up with some startling imagery: four horses of different colors with their riders concerned with apocalyptic woes (N). The first woe is signified by a *white horse* and the *bow* of the rider. Earlier, we were told that Christ was armed with *a sharp two-edged sword* (1:16): the word which comes forth from the Word of God. This conqueror rides the *white horse* of victory, but his victory brings about wanton killing (v. 4), famine (v. 6), and consignment to Hades (v. 8). Christ's victorious ride on his white horse (19:11) brings about the revelation of his name: *King of kings and Lord of lords* (19:16). He does this through his power as *the Word of God* (19:13).

6:3-4 The bright red horse is symbolic of war and the bloodshed due to war. The rider has the authority to take away *peace from the earth* and to incite revolt among the community of humankind. So very different from the message of God's *peace* granted to the churches at the beginning of the work (1:4).

6:5-6 The *black horse* with a *balance* is symbolic of famine. The balance was used for measuring grain. The context speaks of wheat and barley. There was a famine as a result of the black horse, but it was not such as to cause death. A denarius was the going day's wage; *three quarts of barley for a denarius* would indicate that a man would be able to support a small family even during the times of famine. Barley was not considered as desirous as wheat; but one could still live on it. We know that in 92 A.D. the Emperor Domitian decreed that no new vineyard could be planted in Italy and that half of those in the provinces be rooted up and be supplanted by the sowing and growing of grain to alleviate the threat of famine.

6:7-8 The *pale horse* with its grisly riders is symbolic of death. The word *pale* would literally be rendered as *pale green*. In other words, it is corpse colored. This horse wreaks havoc on a *fourth of the earth*. We will see that the various devastating forces become more and more universal as the Book continues. Those affected become greater both in numbers and in areas of the earth. *Death* would be welcome for many since all know that they are bound to die. But this death is not the natural death, but one which comes from the *sword, famine, pestilence* and *wild beasts*. But *Death* is not the end of the grim procession of the four horsemen, for seated behind him is *Hades*: Sheol, Gehenna, the nether world. Yet, the faithful follower of the Lamb need have nothing to fear, for he is told that *Hades* will be thrown into the lake of fire (20:14) with *Death* itself. The Christian has been called to the *marriage supper of the Lamb* (19:9). The Roman Empire cannot harm him or her irreparably.

6:9-11 Those who have died naturally or have been killed in the great persecutions inaugurated by the Romans are still alive. *Those who had been slain* is the same expression used of the standing Lamb (5:6). The devoted followers have suffered the same lot as their master. They implore God to avenge them on *those who dwell on the earth* (3:10). Those who have gone before are nestled under the altar of heaven; they are given protection under the Christ symbol of the altar. They wear the white robe of victory (3:5); they arc told to *rest* for they have earned it (Heb 4:10). Others must still

suffer in order to join them. God's plan must still be unravelled.
6:12-17 With the opening of the sixth seal, the whole of the
universe trembles. Seven created physical things are affected:
earthquake, sun, full moon, the stars, the sky, the mountains, and
the islands. None of God's enemies can escape, for they have no
place to hide. Seven categories of humanity are affected. *kings,*
great men, the strong, the generals, the rich, slave and *free. Wrath*
of the Lamb is a strange expression. It should not be forgotten that
the Lamb is also the Lion of Judah (5:5); it is he who will punish
those who refuse to repent and continue to make war on his people.
No matter what station in life to which they belonged, they will not
be able to escape his wrath; those who dwell upon the earth are
those who will not be able to escape (3:10).

The entire background of this chapter seems to have been
inspired by: Mk 13 of the NT (the Marcan Apocalypse), and by Ezk
5:12-17 and Hab 3:4-15 of the OT.

The question raised in the last verse as to who can stand before
the Lamb's wrath will be answered with the beautiful c. 7.

CHAPTER 7

THE VISION OF THE SAINTS

7:1 All of c. 7 is an interlude between the opening of the sixth seal (6:12) and the seventh seal (8:1). God is holding evil in check by having the four angels hold the winds in check. In 20:8 the evil nations will be gathered from the four corners of the earth. Here, the four angels prevent the winds of the East from damaging earth, sea or trees. The winds seem to be another symbol of the four horsemen of c. 6. The sirocco winds from the deserts of the East can wreak havoc upon the rest of nature even in this day and age.

7:2-3 Rising of the sun: rising is the same word in Greek as the word *East* in Mt 2:1. The East is the place from which blessings come, for it is perceived as the source of all light. This angel has been given the power to seal the *servants of our God*. It should be noted that the angels are fellow servants of God along with humanity. The God of the servants is also the God of the angels. This seal is for protection against the wrath of the Lamb (6:17). In Ex 12:21-27 it was the blood of the Passover lamb which became the protecting agent against the avenging angel. In our text the seal is put on the foreheads of God's servants so that they are easily recognizable. There seems to be a relationship to the *mark* (Hebrew letter *tau*) in Ex 9:4. If one were to envision this mark, it would probably be like some kind of tattoo. This mark or seal indicates already that the Christian is under the powerful name of God, of the Lamb and the New Jerusalem (3:12).

7:4-8 The number of the sealed is 144,000. This is a product of 12 multiplied by 12 multiplied by 1000 (F). It signifies a large undetermined number. Judah is listed first because the *Lion of Judah, the root of David, has conquered* (5:5). We have listed the twelve tribes of Israel with one noticeable alteration. Manasseh (v. 6) is a sub-tribe of Joseph (v. 8). Dan, which was one of the original twelve tribes, has been omitted; but the author needs twelve to indicate the fullness of the OT people of God, and so Manasseh has been substituted. There was a legend circulating at the time that Dan would be the tribe from which the Antichrist would arise. Our author, knowing the legend, cannot permit Dan to be numbered among the twelve and so adds Manasseh. These five vv. in Greek are of great poetic beauty.

7:9-12 Now we have the *great multitude* in heaven from every nation. They are already wearing the robes of victory and carrying the sign of victory, palm branches, in their hands. They have come from every *nation, tribe, people,* and *tongue*; as it were, from the four corners of the earth. Jesus' triumphal entry into Jerusalem had been heralded by the palm branches (Jn 12:13). In c. 5, the song sung had been about worthiness; now the song is about *salvation* which has been brought about by God and the Lamb. Again there are seven adjectives of praise used to honor God in v. 12.

7:13-17 The dramatic character of the book again unfolds in the dialog between John and one of the elders. The elder asks the question as to the identity of all these people in heaven. John replies in words which could be rendered as follows in order to convey their meaning: "Mr. Elder, you live here in heaven; you ought to know the answer to your own question better than I. After all, I'm just a visitor." The elder's reply is magnificent in its beauty of the mixed metaphor of washing robes in order to make them white in the blood of the Lamb. Those in heaven are there because they followed Jesus fully in all that he had given them to do; they are victorious with him only because they gave of themselves. Only a living active faith which totally possesses the person, and not merely the intellect, can bring one to wear the white robe of victory. These people have arrived at the end of the final exodus, their pilgrimage to the heavenly city. There are seven things which the Lord will do for them in heaven: *shelter them with his presence*; *they will hunger no more*; *they will not be thirsty*; *the sun shall not strike them nor any scorching heat*; *the Lamb will be their shepherd*; *he will guide them to springs of living water*; and *God will wipe away every tear from their eyes*. It was during the Exodus led by Moses that the people had suffered in the desert on their way to the Promised Land. Now, having arrived at the true home, the heavenly city, God will care for all of his faithful followers' needs. He even takes out his handkerchief to enter into a personal relationship with his people to wipe away their tears from their eyes. There is no permanent dwelling for us here below; *we seek the city which is to come* (Heb 13:14).

THE FIRST FOUR TRUMPETS SOUND

8:1-2 In every celebration, there is the need for silence to reflect upon what has been occuring and to prepare for what will come next. Thus, the opening of the last seal brings this restful silence which the author tells us lasted *for about half an hour*. In the Bible, silence has theological importance: Hab 2:20; Zc 2:17; Zp 1:7-8. The seven angels are known to us through extra-biblical sources as well as through the Bible. Raphael is known to us from the Book of Tobit; Michael from the Books of Daniel, Revelation, and Jude; Gabriel from the Books of Daniel and Luke. The remaining four come from extra-biblical sources (1 Enoch 20). Their names are Uriel, Raguel, Sariel and Remiel. The *el* portion of each name is a Hebrew word for God; each angel somehow manifests God's works.

8:3-5 In 6:9-11 we saw the saints under the altar of heaven praying for God to intervene and avenge their blood. In 5:8 the elders of heaven held golden bowls of incense in their hands *which are the prayers of the saints*. In our vv., the imagery has changed and now the incense is wrath-filled and directed toward the punishment of the earth. The censer is filled with *fire* from the altar and is thrown upon the earth; there are four phenomena which occur: *peals of thunder, loud noises, flashes of lightning* and *an earthquake*. In Dn 7:11-12, fire is used to destroy God's enemies as here it comes down from heaven.

8:6-7   In 6:8 a fourth of the earth had been harmed. The destruction becomes more pervasive here, for one third is now affected. These and the following vv. seem to have their origin in the plagues which afflicted Egypt (Ex 9:23, 25; 7:17-21; 10:21-23). The trumpet, then as now, was used to herald great events.

8:8-12   With the second, third and fourth trumpets there is a continuation of the affliction of the earth in terms of one third: sea, sea creatures, ships, rivers, sun, moon, stars, fountains of water. In each of the four trumpets, three things have been touched after their sounding. Thus, once again the significance of the numbers 3, 4 and 12 is highlighted. *Wormwood* is a plant which has a bitter taste. It was used for poisoning the water of the false prophets (Jr 23:15). In times of military conquest, it would have the function of poisoning the water supply of the enemy.

8:13   There is a brief interlude of an eagle crying out a triple woe *to those who dwell on the earth* (N). No Christians make a permanent home upon the earth. The persecutors do not yet know of any other possible home, and have made their permanent dwelling place here. The first four trumpets had inaugurated destruction upon material creation; the woes upon human beings. One can picture the solitary eagle circling above and uttering his terrible prediction. Some Bible manuscripts have alternate readings for the word *eagle*. Some read *vulture* and some *angel*. The best rendering appears to be *eagle* as we have in the text. In Biblical literature, *eagle* is often used as an image for an invading army (Hab 1:8). In our text the word *eagle* may refer to the Roman Army, since the imperial standard always bore an eagle as a symbol of Rome. In this case, the army would be used as God's instrument. In Ex 19:4, God told the Israelites that he led them out of Egypt as though borne on eagle's wings. If God is pictured as the eagle here, then he has changed that imagery of Exodus and is now about to chastise the persecutors of his people. It should be remembered that one of the living creatures has a face like a *flying eagle* (4:7).

CHAPTER 9

THE ABOMINABLE LOCUST- AND HORSE-LIKE BEASTS

9:1-2 A *star fallen from heaven* may well indicate Satan. The Greek verb is a perfect tense and indicates the past. Jesus says that he saw Satan fall like a star from heaven (Lk 10:18). (The ancients believed that the stars were living creatures.) *Bottomless pit* or *abyss* is mentioned seven times in our Book (9:1, 2, 11; 11:7; 17:8; 20:1, 3). It was often identified with the lowest part of Gehenna. Gehenna had originally been the garbage dump of Jerusalem, where there was a constant burning of refuse. Thus, smoke and fire came to be associated with the *bottomless pit* or *hell* as it is known today.

9:3-6 These locust beasts with the stings of scorpions are told not to harm the earth, and only to torment those who had not the *seal of God upon their foreheads* (7:3). The five-month period refers to the normal length of a locust plague: the last five months of the Jewish year. A plague of locusts was looked upon as the result of God's displeasure (Dt 28:38). Some commentators see all of cc. 8-9 as referring to the historical circumstances which preceded the Roman destruction of the city of Jerusalem in 70 A.D.—albeit by use of apocalyptic language. The locust plague finds its clearest antecedent in the plagues of Egypt (Ex 10:12-15).

9:7-11 Jl 2:4-11 is the source from which our author has drawn his conflated description. Our vv. render a most horrendous description of these bellicose beasts. These locust-horse beasts possessed their sting in their tails. And again they afflicted men for five months. *Abbadon* is used synonymously with Sheol in Job 28:22. It is also the poetic word for the lowest part of Gehenna. The angel of the bottomless pit is Satan (R).

9:12-19 The *horns* of the altar in heaven suggest God's power. There were horns upon the altar of sacrifice in the Jewish Temple. The second and third woes will be mentioned in 11:14. The river Euphrates is the longest one in Western Asia; it is often considered as the cradle of civilization. It served as the boundary between the Roman Empire and the unconquered Parthians. The bellicose description of the horses continues with the recounting of the murder of one third of humanity. The description of v. 17 is dragon-like in character.

9:20-21 The plagues did not seem to have their effect: repentance. The author holds out the possibility of repentance to all human beings, even the nations as such (21:24). Nevertheless, God's chastising activity does not seem to have affected the greed and conduct of the survivors. The worship of demons and idols is the worst of sins; these individuals have placed other gods before them, for they do not follow the Lamb wherever he goes as do the faithful of 14:4.

CHAPTER 10

JOHN ACCEPTS HIS VOCATION TO BE A PROPHET

10:1-3   There is an interruption in the sounding of the trumpets between trumpet six (9:13) and trumpet seven (11:15). The same procedure had been followed between seal six (6:12) and seal seven (8:1). This angel is majestic, standing with one foot in the sea and another on the land similar to the Colossus of Rhodes, which was one of the seven wonders of the ancient world. A rainbow had surrounded God seated on his throne (4:3). A cloud had led the chosen people on the first Exodus during the day and a pillar of fire had led them at night (Ex 13:22). This angel is God's special messenger. The little scroll is not a sealed scroll, and is in marked contrast to the mighty angel.

10:4-7   The angel raises his right hand to heaven and makes an oath. This gesture, together with the fact that he is standing on earth and sea, suggests that he is asking the earth, sea and heaven itself to bear witness, for he calls upon the name of the Creator. Both the imagery and the very words of calling upon the Creator refer the reader to c. 4. It is time for the *mystery of God to be fulfilled*. The mystery is that Christ *shall reign for ever and ever* (11:15), and that Satan has been overthrown (20:10). The angel announces that there will be *no more delay* for these things to come to pass.

10:8-11   Ezekiel also was asked to eat a scroll which would be like honey in his mouth (Ezk 2:8-3:3). Our account is one of contrasts: a great angel, a little scroll. The little scroll should be identified with the NT which Christ has given us. Unlike the seven-sealed scroll which could only have fulfillment with the coming of Christ (i.e., the OT), the little scroll's message is clear to those who will accept it. John has to take it himself; he has to digest it; the message is sweet since it is Jesus Christ. Nevertheless, when he preaches (L), bitterness will come to him, because those to whom he preaches will not readily accept the message. It is the role of the preacher of the Gospel; the sweetness will get him through the bitterness.

CHAPTER 11

DELIVERANCE FOR THE PEOPLE OF GOD

11:1-3 Until this point of the narrative, John had been a spectator. Now, having accepted the scroll and his prophetic vocation, he becomes actively involved in the happenings in the remainder of the Book. The purpose of the measuring is for protection. The outer court of the Jewish Temple was reserved for the Gentiles, whereas the inner court was reserved for the Jews. In one sense, our author is saying that the People of God are those who worship in the true Temple; the persecutors are those outside. Therefore, only the inner court is measured. The numbers which are mentioned, *forty-two months* and *one thousand two hundred and sixty days* find their OT background in Daniel (7:25 and 12:7, *a time, two times and a half time*) (F). In Rv 11:9 there is also a reference to *three and a half days*. During the Maccabean revolt, there was much hardship and tribulation endured during the persecution of Antiochus IV Epiphanes. The persecution broke out in June 168/7 B.C. and ended in December 165/4 B.C.: a period of three and a half years. It was the period of tribulation, but the Jews were delivered after that time. Thus, in our context, 42, 1260, and 3½ are all different ways of expressing a time of tribulation after which God will deliver his people. It should be noted that *those who worship in the temple* are measured and do not suffer from the trampling of the city.

11:4-9 The Lord is the *Lord of the earth* and he has sentinel prophets who do his bidding. Two prophets are depicted like olive trees and lampstands (Zc 4:1-14), because it was necessary for two to bear witness (Dt 19:15). It would seem that they represent Elijah (2 K 1:10) who caused the sky to withold its rain, and Moses (Ex 7:17, 19) who turned the Egyptian rivers into blood. These same two prophets appear with Jesus at his transfiguration (Lk 9:30). Sodom had become proverbial for its immorality (Gn 19) and Egypt for its enslavement of God's people (Ex 1). The demonic powers make war upon the two witnesses, kill them, and dishonor them by not allowing their bodies to be buried. They lie in the street for *three days and a half* (cf. vv. 1-3 above). The *great city* is Jerusalem, the murderer of prophets (Mt 23:37-39).

11:10-13 The spite is so great that *those who dwell on the earth* have a great party, for they have removed the prophets who called them to repentance from their midst. And yet, God wins the day—for after the *three and a half days*, those who murdered them stand in great fear as they see them taken up into heaven. Elijah was taken to heaven in a fiery chariot (2 K 2:11), and in the noncanonical book *The Assumption of Moses*, written around 30 A.D., Moses also was taken up into heaven. Just as Jesus ascended into heaven after having been put to death outside Jerusalem, so too his faithful witnesses. Jerusalem has come to mean not merely the physical city of the Jews, but the city of all who oppose Christ. Nevertheless, there is complete vindication for the witnesses as their enemies must watch them being taken up into heaven, the new Jerusalem (21:2). *Seven thousand* signifies a perfect unlimited amount; *one tenth*, an undetermined amount (F).

11:14-19 The seventh trumpet inaugurates the rule of Christ. This is very important for our author. Christ reigns now; he is now the victorious one. The famous *Hallelujah Chorus* of Handel was inspired by 11:15; 19:6 and 19:16. It captures the mood of our verses: exuberant joy. The twenty-four elders praise God *who is and who was*. He is here, and therefore they do not need to add *is to come* (4:8). God has taken active control of the world and made it a kingdom of the Christ. The *ark of the covenant was seen within his temple*. The ark of the covenant had been seen but once a year and only by the high priest, on the occasion of the Day of Atonement. Now, with Christ, the ark which represents God's presence in the midst of his people can be approached by everyone. Christ has begun his reign. This vision of the temple in heaven is somewhat symbolic; we are told in 21:22 that in the New Jerusalem there will be no temple, for its *temple is the Lord God the Almighty and the Lamb*.

CHAPTER 12

THE WOMAN CLOTHED WITH THE SUN

12:1-2 The word *portent* is a translation for *semeion*, sign, and is used seven times in Revelation. This, then, is the first of the seven signs; the others are to be found in 12:3; 13:13,14; 15:1; 16:14 and 19:20. This is the only positive sign; the remaining six deal with the beast or with destruction upon the earth. *Woman* or the plural form *women* is found 19 times in the Book. It should be noted that this woman is clothed with heavenly ornaments: the *sun*, the *moon*, the *stars*. She is in sharp contrast to the woman of c. 17, the harlot of Babylon. The woman is in *anguish for delivery* of her child. However, she has other offspring (v. 17). It would seem that the *woman* is the community of believers from whom the Messiah came: first of all, the OT people of God; and then the NT people of God which has given birth to countless brothers and sisters of Jesus Christ. In the first instance, the woman is not Mary, Mother of the God-Man, Jesus. The mentioning of *twelve stars* should be noted as well.

12:3-4 We now come to the second sign, the *great red dragon. Dragon* (R) appears only in Rv where it occurs twelve times. The dragon is that *ancient serpent, who is called the Devil and Satan* (v. 9). There is no doubt that our author is depicting the force of darkness arrayed against the people of God. The *seven heads and ten horns* prefigure the sea beast's *ten horns and seven heads* (T) (13:1). The sea beast will be seen as the actual incarnation of the evil of the dragon. The power of the dragon is tremendous. For this reason he can wreak havoc upon the *stars of heaven*.

12:5-6 In Gn 3:15 we have the recounting of the enmity between the serpent and the woman (Eve). Here there is another encounter between the devil and humanity. The dragon wishes to destroy the male child, the Messiah. The royal Psalm 2:9 is quoted: *she brought forth a male child, one who is to rule all the nations with a rod of iron*. In the glorification of Christ who has ascended to the throne of God in heaven, Satan is defeated. The woman flees to the wilderness after her child has been caught up to God's throne. The wilderness was understood to be a place of safety. The 1260 (F) days is considered the time of tribulation during which the Christian community will be bombarded by evil. It is the same as the 42 months and the 3½ days (11:2,11) and *a time, and times and half a time* (12:14). With the exaltation of Christ in heaven, the Christian community is still being nourished upon the earth under God's protection.

12:7-9 Herein we have depicted the casting out of Satan and his angels from the heavenly realm. Michael is shown as the leader of God's armies against the Devil and his cohorts. In Hebrew, *Michael* means "one who is like God." He is mentioned in our text and in Jude 9 and Dn 10:13,21 and 12:1. He was considered to be a kind of patron saint of Israel, and was supposed to lead Israel in battle against evil on the last day. Satan appears as the prosecutor in the heavenly court (Jb 1:6ff). Michael is presented as the defense lawyer for the Christians. Because Christ has been glorified and *caught up to God and to his throne* (v. 5), Michael proclaims the victory, *fighting* (*polemesai* from which we get the English word *polemics*). We should not envision an actual gruesome battle. Satan is powerless before God's throne.

12:10-12 We are reminded that Christ actually reigns. He is reigning during the persecution of Domitian, during which time the Book was written. And we know that he continues to reign now. It is because of Christ's authority that *the accuser of our brethren has been thrown down*. The *blood of the Lamb* has given the *brethren* the power to conquer, for it is the victorious blood of the redemption which has made their personal witness and testimony fruitful. Satan cannot harm or threaten those in heaven. He can tempt those upon the earth and the sea, but even there he is limited; *his time is short*.

12:13-14   Daniel speaks of *a time, two times and a half time*: a reference to the three and a half years of troubled times during the Maccabean persecution. The Church, the Christian community, is nourished in the wilderness for the same period of time. In Ex 19:4 Yahweh reminds his people that he has led them on eagle's wings. It would seem that God leads the Church here to a place of safety, with that same imagery of an eagle's wings.

12:15-18   The emphasis here is placed upon the serpent-dragon and his constant harassment of the woman's offspring. The reference to water and the flood in v. 15 might also go back to the Exodus Event when the Pharaoh was likened to *the great dragon that lies in the midst of his streams* (Ezk 29:3). The earth is seen as an agent of God in Nb 26:10 and in Dt 11:6 and in Ps 106:16-18 where the sacred authors recount how God punished Dathan and Abiram by having the earth swallow them up. Here, God has the earth swallow the flood so that the woman would remain safe. *And he stood on the sand of the sea* (v. 17) is a foretaste of what will be, with the introduction of evil become incarnate in the sea beast of c. 13.

CHAPTER 13

THE SEA AND LAND BEASTS

13:1 This introduces us to the infamous beast whose number is *six hundred and sixty-six* (v. 18). This beast is the raw political power of the Roman Empire which sent its armies across the Mediterranean Sea in ships to attack and conquer the peoples of Asia Minor (modern day Turkey). The *seven heads* most likely refer to the seven Roman Emperors beginning with Nero, the first persecutor of the Christians, and culminating in Domitian, who was currently persecuting the faithful of Asia Minor. The *ten horns* would refer to kingly power. The author is drawing upon the OT Book of Daniel, where in 7:24 a beast with ten horns signifies various kings opposed to God's people. A *blasphemous name* would refer to the Emperors who took it upon themselves to be called divine, who made themselves into gods.

13:2-3 The beast is described in terms of the four beasts found in Dn 7. In Dn 7 there are four separate beasts. Here there is but one beast, a composite of the four in Dn. The beasts in Dn are oppressors of God's people. There was a legend about the Emperor Nero (A) which claimed that he would some day come back to life. This legend circulated in ancient times. In one sense, the author of Revelation is saying that the first persecutor of the Church has returned to life in the present persecution under Domitian. Thus, *one of its heads seemed to have a mortal wound, but its mortal wound was healed.*

13:4-8 These verses describe the activity of this beast from the sea. *Those who dwell in heaven* is found in 7:15; 12:12; 13:6; 21:3 and signifies just the opposite of *those who dwell on the earth* (11:10). The faithful Christian is called to live in heaven; that is where the permanent dwelling or (literally) *tabernacle* is found. Thus, the beast blasphemes God, his name and his home as well as those who are already with him in heaven. Those who make their permanent dwelling here below, *those who dwell on earth*, are the ones who worship the Emperor and not God. *The book of life of the Lamb that was slain* signifies that the Christian's name is written in heaven; humanity belongs to God and not to any Emperor. The *forty-two months* is a period of tribulation, a period which will endure as long as the Church remains upon the earth and has not seen all of its members arrive safely to their heavenly home.

13:9-10 These verses are a compilation of Jr 15:2 and Mt 26:52, and bespeak the necessity of suffering imprisonment or death for one's faith, as the case may be. Verse 9 is similar to the admonition found at the end of the letters to the seven churches (e.g., 3:22).

13:11-15 The second beast *out of the earth* is introduced. This is a land beast which *had two horns like a lamb and it spoke like a dragon*. This beast is false religion (R) which tries to pass itself off as authentic religion under the guise of a lamb, the symbol of true religion in Revelation. Lk mentions the Asiarchs in Ac 19:31. The Asiarchs had the duty of enforcing the practice of Emperor worship in Asia Minor. This beast is a land beast who is later called the false prophet (16:13; 19:20; 20:10). He is subservient to the sea beast, the political power of the Roman Empire. What we have is a trinity of evil with the dragon, sea beast and land beast arrayed against the Christian community. As false religion, the land beast is involved in magical practices. The legend of Nero coming back to life is again alluded to in v. 14. Those who would not perform their civic duty of offering worship to the Emperor were put to death.

13:16-18 These are some of the best known verses in the book. It would seem that those who actually did perform their duty of offering true worship to the Emperor would be given some type of identification mark to prove to authorities that they had performed their obligation. Christians, who would not have had this special identification, would have been excluded from the economic life of the country, not being permitted to *buy* or *sell*. The author tells us that this is a human number: 666. Thus, it is the name of some well-known person. 666 in Hebrew numerals signifies *Nero Caesar* (G).

CHAPTER 14

THE LAMB ON MOUNT ZION

14:1-5   Mt. Zion was the place where the OT prophets believed that God would restore the faithful remnant and make them into a mighty people in Messianic times (Jl 3:5). Note that the Lamb stands on a mountain in an exalted place; the beast had come slithering out of the sea (13:1). In c. 7 the author had spoken about the remnant of Israel with the twelve thousand from each of the twelve tribes. We have already said that *a hundred and forty-four thousand* should be considered as an unlimited perfect number. Those who follow the Lamb do not need the *mark* of the beast. They have the Lamb's *and his Father's name written on their foreheads*. They once again sing a new song (5:9), and we are reminded of the triumphant liturgical worship of heaven. Only the redeemed can sing this new song. They *have not defiled themselves with women, for they are chaste*: this is a statement which once again insists upon the practice of true religion, of following the Lamb-Jesus. So often in the ancient Near East, false religious practices involved the practice of sacred prostitution in fertility rituals. To practice true religion would signify that the individual was chaste. Thus the term *chaste* should be understood in its proper religious context of fidelity to true religion, and not understood as the virtue of chastity. . . . *And in their mouth no lie was found, for they are spotless*: the word for *spotless* is the proper Greek word used in the Greek translation of the OT for suitable victims for sacrifice. In giving their lives (P) for their faith in Jesus, these Christians, united with the Lamb, have been accepted as suitable sacrifices unto the Lord.

14:6-12 The last angel to be mentioned was the one who blew the seventh trumpet in 11:15. Now three other angels are introduced. They are concerned about the eternal good news or *eternal gospel* which is being proclaimed. These verses look forward to the fall of Rome: *Fallen, fallen is Babylon the great*—which is once more reiterated in 18:2 even before Babylon has been introduced in 17:5. The eternal message is directed to all peoples, for it is a universal message. It is a message which demands a choice: giving glory to God (v. 7) or being tormented (v. 10). Raw political power, Rome under the guise of the image of Babylon (where the chosen people had languished in exile, 586-536 B.C.), will not prevail against God's wrath (v. 10).

4:13 This is the second of the seven beatitudes which are contained in Revelation (cf. commentary for 1:3). *Deeds follow them*: one of the criteria for being included in the great judgment books in heaven: *And the dead were judged by what was written in the books, by what they had done* (20:12).

14:14-16 The time of harvest for the faithful individuals is presented. In 1:7 our author had pointed out that Jesus was about to come upon the clouds. Now we see *one like a son of man coming* upon a cloud; he is the same individual who was seen walking in the midst of the seven lampstands in 1:13. The *earth was reaped*; the faithful had been ready to stand up to the Roman Empire because of their faith. Elsewhere, Jesus had told his disciples that the fields had been made ready for the harvest (Jn 4:35). Now we are told that it was God's plan for the faithful to lose their lives for the sake of Christ, in order that they might gain a continuous new life. In the immediate persecution of the saints in Domitian's day, a further explanation had been given to the saints who were resting under the altar in heaven (6:9-11). These now *were to be killed as they themselves had been* (6:11).

14:17-19   The wicked are punished. *One like a son of man* (v. 14) does not do the punishing, but an angel (v. 19) does.
Jesus had suffered outside the city gates (Heb 13:12-14). Now we are told that his enemies will be trodden *outside the city* (v. 20). *One thousand six hundred stadia* is equivalent to approximately two hundred miles. All of this is an anticipation of the final victory, which our author will treat in c. 19 with the man on the white horse.

CHAPTER 15

THE SONG OF THE LAMB

15:1-2 Herein is mentioned the fourth sign or *portent*, in the sevenfold list: 12:3; 13:13,14; 15:1; 16:14; 19:20. The *seven plagues* inaugurate devastations similar to those found in Ex 7ff., and hearken back to Lv 26:21: *Then if you walk contrary to me, and will not hearken to me, I will bring more plagues upon you, sevenfold as many as your sins.* A *sea of glass* had first been presented in heaven (4:6) in an earlier episode. It is presented as a place of refuge for those who have conquered; it is very different from the sea from which the beast arose in 13:1. The conquerors are singing. Heaven is filled with song.

15:3-4 Here we see how the *song of Moses* (H) has been transformed. It is now the *song of the Lamb*. Moses had led his people through the desert on the way to a place of safety; he had led them out of Egypt. The Lamb, Jesus, is the new leader of the pilgrim people and he has led them to a place of safety: heaven. Moses' song had first been sung on the banks of the Sea of Reeds after deliverance from the Pharaoh's armies (Ex 15:1-18). Jesus has led the faithful Christians dryshod into heaven; they are safe from the beast. The song sung is one of praise of the Lord God the Almighty.

15:5-8 The *seven plagues* with their impending destruction, are introduced. The expression *tent of witness* is found in one other place in the NT, and that is in Ac 7:44. The word *witness* translates a Greek word from which we derive the English word, *martyr.* The whole of c. 15 is speaking about the peace and tranquility of the Christian martyrs in heaven who are in God's sanctuary. Much of the imagery of this section takes us back to the heavenly throne room of cc. 4-5 except that instead of the singing of songs, there is the unleashing of plagues upon God's enemies (N).

CHAPTER 16

THE SEVEN BOWLS OF WRATH

Throughout this chapter, there is a reiteration of the various plagues which had afflicted Egypt. With the plagues, there are also the attendant themes of destruction. The plagues and destruction call to mind the two geographical sites of 11:8: *Sodom and Egypt*. The plagues of Egypt are treated in Ex 7:17-12:32. The destruction of Sodom is mentioned in Gn 19:24.

16:1-2 It is pointed out that the destruction in this chapter is directed to all who *bore the mark of the beast and worshipped its name*. The faithful have *conquered the beast and its image and the number of its name* (15:2).

16:3-7 The destruction motif is continued. However, vv. 5-7 are in poetry once again. Retribution has been meted out to the enemies of the Lamb who have been given *blood to drink*. In v. 7 those under the altar (6:9-11) cry out in a song of victory. *Yea, Lord God the Almighty, true and just are thy judgments!*

16:8-11 These verses demonstrate the resistance of those signed with the mark of the beast to God's chastisements: *they did not repent* (vv. 9, 11). Instead of repenting, these individuals even curse God (vv. 9, 11).

16:12-16 These are among the most quoted in the work. The *Euphrates* and the Tigris are two rivers in modern-day Iraq, whose environs are called the cradle of civilization. They flow into the Persian Gulf. Babylon was located on the Euphrates. Cyrus the

Great drained and blocked up the river so that he might successfully capture the city in the 6th century B.C. Verse 13 depicts an evil triumvirate: the dragon, the beast and the false prophet (the land beast of v. 13). They are unclean creatures. This is highlighted with the note that frog-like spirits come forth from their mouths. Frogs were considered as unclean animals by the Jews. We have the third beatitude in v. 15. *Armageddon* (v. 16) is said to be the place for the great battle. Most commentators would understand it to mean the mountain of Megiddo (S). No such place as Armageddon is found on any map of the ancient world.

16:17-20   This scene appears to recapture the destruction of the city of Jerusalem by Titus in the year 70 A.D. There had been three Jewish leaders, Simon bar Giora, Eleazar the Zealot and John of Gischala. This may account for the description of v. 17 that *the great city was split into three parts*. These verses are at one and the same time applied to the Roman Empire. The same type of destruction was to occur to them as they had wreaked on the earthly Jerusalem. *Hailstones, heavy as a hundredweight* would weigh about one hundred and thirty pounds. In ancient warfare, this type of weight would be hurled by the catapults against the walls of a besieged city. Nevertheless, all this apparent destruction does not bring about conversion. Just the opposite is true: *men cursed God for the plague of the hail* (v. 21).

CHAPTER 17

THE GREAT HARLOT

17:1-2 We are introduced to the great harlot with whom *the dwellers on earth have become drunk.* Those who make their permanent dwelling upon the earth are those who are the enemies of the Lamb and his followers (cf. 3:8-11). Harlotry is another way of speaking about idolatry, because false religion always involved some type of sacred prostitution in the ancient world (cf. 14:1-5). This harlot is opposed and contrasted with the *woman clothed with the sun* (12:1). The harlot has entered into relationships with the *kings of the earth*, vassal and allied kings with the Roman Empire.

17:3-6 This is a description of the harlot woman. This woman is seated upon a *scarlet beast which was full of blasphemous names. Blasphemy* is to indicate that a creature is really God. This is what had happened in the Roman Empire when the Emperors had been divinized and called "God" and "Savior." The woman is the corporate person who epitomizes all that was corrupt in the Roman Empire. The phrase, *Babylon the great, mother of harlots and earth's abominations* comes down to us in the Greek manuscripts of Revelation in capital letters. This is most unusual in what are called minuscule manuscripts, in which all the letters are lower case. By every letter being upper case in this phrase, the author is pointing out a title of importance to the reader. The only other occurrence of this in Revelation is to be found in 19:16. This woman, who is called *Babylon*, has become drunk with the *blood of the saints and the blood of the martyrs of Jesus*. She is, in fact, drunk with the blood of the offspring of the woman of c. 12. In c. 12, those offspring had conquered *by the blood of the Lamb and by the word of their testimony, for they loved not their lives even unto death* (12:11). The woman of c. 17 is responsible for their deaths. This woman then, in the first instance is not a specific woman, but rather the Roman Empire itself. Nevertheless, just as Mary, the mother of Jesus, stands behind the image of the people of God in c. 12, so too here a woman stands behind the image of the Roman Empire. That woman would be the harlot wife of Claudius (41-54 A.D.), Valeria Messalina, whom the Emperor put to death because of her public harlotry. She came to epitomize all that was corrupt in the Roman Empire. Her harlotry was remembered by the Roman writers Juvenal and Tacitus many years after her shameful death. Juvenal speaks about her in his *Satires* (c. 110-130 A.D.) and Tacitus in his *Annals* (c. 150 A.D.).

17:7-8 These verses give the same picture as 13:1, 3 with the naming of the *beast with seven heads and ten horns* (G). The beast *was and is not and is to come*; this is once again an allusion to the legend that Nero, the first Emperor to persecute the Christians, was to come back to life again some day. That day was the time of the writer of our work, for he understood that Nero had come back in the person of his successor, the Roman Emperor Domitian, who was persecuting the Christian community. The *book of life* has already been mentioned in 13:8 and will be seen again in 20:12, 15.

17:9-11 We are given an explanation of the previous picture. The same thing occured in 1:20 where an explanation was given about the previous vision of one like a son of man. The *seven heads are seven mountains*: a clear reference to the famous seven hills of the city of Rome. They are also said to be *seven kings*; the author is using the number seven for his own purposes (F), signifying seven of the Roman Emperors (T). *An eighth* would signify Domitian and the legend of Nero come back to life.

17:12-14 The author speaks about the future as relative to his own day. The *ten horns* symbolize *ten kings* who will receive power from the beast. That power, however, will be short-lived since it will last but one hour. Nevertheless, they are allies with the beast to fight against the Lamb. But the Lamb together with his *chosen and faithful* followers will prove to be victorious. The Lamb is the greatest lord and the greatest king (cf. 19:16).

17:15-18   Here is pointed out the final outcome of the harlot's endeavor. Evil will turn in upon itself and destroy the harlot. The evil of Imperial Rome would be destroyed by its own allies and from within. The *great city* which makes itself great in opposition to God's dominion will destroy itself. This is the lot of all powers inimical to God.

CHAPTER 18

IN ANTICIPATION, BABYLON-ROME IS DESTROYED

Most of this chapter is in poetry, and much is reminiscent of the recounting of the fall of the Prince of Tyre (Ezk 28). Adjectives are heaped up, and nouns as well, in order to point out the impending doom of the persecutor Babylon-Rome. God's people will not suffer continuously from the hated oppressor.

18:1-3 Here we see that Babylon is indeed a fallen city. Its wealth was not sufficient to save it from itself. It has become *a haunt of every foul spirit*. The word *foul* means unclean. Although the Christians had been considered as *first fruits* and *spotless* sacrifices (14:4, 5) in the giving of their lives, Babylon has become a place for the *foul*, the unclean. Those who had died there were not found suitable for the Lord.

18:4-8 Once again the pride of Babylon is depicted. She was arrogant, and so she must pay for her misdeeds with a *double draught*. She had drunk *the blood of the martyrs of Jesus* (17:6). Now she must drink a double portion of her own misdeeds.

18:9-16 These verses point out how the merchant class wails at the impending destruction of Babylon, because their economic life has also been ruined. The earth has been laid waste, and earthly gain has suffered.

18:17-19 The sea, too, has been affected. So much of commerce was conducted through trade ships. The sea and those who use it

join the merchants of the earth to wail, because they have lost out
on economic opportunity.

18:20-24   This is a summary of the chapter. Those in heaven
rejoice, because she who had attempted to make herself a god has
been destroyed. Babylon-Rome has been destroyed because she
was found guilty of *the blood of prophets and of saints* (cf.
11:4-10). She will be as desolate as was Jerusalem of old, when the
voice of the *bridegroom and bride* were no longer heard in the land
(Jr 25:10).

CHAPTER 19

KING OF KINGS AND LORD OF LORDS

19:1-3 Herein are inaugurated the peals of victory for the Lamb. *A great multitude in heaven* break into song (H). The accordion effect mentioned in 5:8-14 finds its fulfillment in this chapter. The song had gone forth from the throne in c. 5, and now in c. 19 it returns to the throne. Handel's oratorio *The Messiah* found the basis for the *Hallelujah Chorus* in 11:15, 19:6 and 19:16. In our vv. the *hallelujahs* resound in praise of God.

19:4-5 This is the last appearance of the twenty-four elders. But from the multitude to the elders, the song has come back to God. God is victorious and therefore there is the shout, *Praise our God, all you his servants.*

19:6-8 The reader is introduced to *the marriage of the Lamb* and *his Bride.* The bride is the Christian community, and the Lamb is Jesus. This relationship of Christ as husband and the Church as bride is also found in Ep 5:28-30. The bride is clothed in the radiance of heaven, *bright and pure.* Her clothing is, in fact, the *righteous deeds* of her members. Earlier (14:13), we were told that the deeds of those who have died do indeed follow them. Now we are reminded that their righteous deeds have furnished the clothing for the Church. The saints *have washed their robes and made them white in the blood of the Lamb* (7:14).

19:9-10 Another one of the beatitudes is pointed out. *Blessed are those who are invited to the marriage supper of the Lamb* are the exact words, in the Latin original, of the text used in Catholic ritual before the communion rite in the Eucharistic celebration. The joys of heaven are mirrored already now in the table fellowship of the Christian community. Verse 10 deals with a polemic against angel worship. In the early Church, some Christians were influenced by pagan forces and had such a high regard for angels that they began to worship them as gods. John is reminding the Christians of his day that there is but one God, and that even angels are creatures. This same polemic is found in 22:8-9.

19:11-15 These verses are extremely important for understanding the theology of Revelation. Verse 11 speaks about *heaven opened*. In 4:1 there was an *open door* in heaven; in 11:19 *God's temple in heaven was opened*. Now it is heaven itself which is opened. The rider is seated upon a *white horse*; his identity will be made known in v. 16; the imagery here is not the same as that found in 6:2. *His eyes are like a flame of fire* (1:14). In 12:3 the dragon wore seven diadems and in 13:1 the sea beast wore ten. The one on a *white horse* wears *many diadems*. His name is a secret one. "Name" signifies the entire person; he reveals who he is in v. 16. Considering the unity of the book, the blood in the expression *a robe dipped in blood*, is the blood of the rider. The rider is the same as the *Lamb standing, as though it had been slain* (5:6). He is the same individual about whom the throngs of heaven sing that his *blood didst ransom men for God* (5:9). Blood is life (Gn 9:4); the rider has given his lifeblood, and it is through his blood that he reveals who he is. Seated upon a horse, *a robe dipped in blood* would be at the eye level of a footman. He is called *the Word of God* (v. 13). In 1:16 *one like a son of man* had a *sharp two-edged sword* issuing from his mouth. That sword is his word; it is his only armament; his word convicts, convinces and exonerates. In 19:13 he is called *the Word of God*; thus, a sharp sword issues from his mouth (v. 15). *Rod of iron* comes from Ps 2:9.

19:16 We know who the rider really is. His name is inscribed on *his robe and on his thigh*. The name is at eye level. The best Greek manuscripts once again have handed down to us the expression *King of kings and Lord of lords* in all upper case, capital letters. It is a title. It is he who has indeed conquered the harlot Babylon (17:5). He is the only answer to her title (U).

19:17-21 These verses catalogue the defeat of God's enemies, who are also naturally enough the Christians' enemies. The sea beast (v. 20) was captured and so is the land beast who is called the *false prophet* (v. 20); false prophecy is false religion which tries to pass itself off as true. Thus, we see that the King of kings and Lord of lords has destroyed two of the great enemies of all humanity.

CHAPTER 20

SATAN IS DEFEATED

20:1-3 These verses speak about the thousand years of Satan being chained. Verse 7 tells of Satan being loosed after the thousand years. These thousand years are called the millennium (D, E, J). The beast from the sea and the false prophet have already been thrown *into the lake of fire that burns with sulphur* (19:20). It is now the time for Satan to be sentenced. The *bottomless pit* or *abyss* is mentioned in the following vv.: 9:1, 2,11; 11:7; 17:8; 20:1, 3. We see that Satan has been *chained* (v. 1), but later he will be *loosed* (v. 3). Satan had already been cast from heaven, and could no longer in any way accuse humanity before God's throne (12:7-9). He has no power over Christians, for there is only one Lord who reigns (v. 4). Verses 1-3 are parallel vith vv. 4-6, for they take place contemporaneously.

20:4-6 We are informed about the reign of the saints with Christ. Satan has been chained by the redeeming blood of the *Lamb standing, as though it had been slain* (5:6). Satan and his followers have been vanquished by the *King of kings and Lord of lords* (19:16). The last days have already been inaugurated, and have continued since the coming of Christ until the present moment: *in these last days he has spoken to us by his Son* (Heb 1:2). The *first resurrection* concerns the faithful who have suffered and died for the Lord and now live with him. The *second death* is not physical death; rather, it is condemnation to the bottomless pit. *A thousand years* simply signifies a long undetermined period of time. Those who practice true religion, and had not received the mark of the beast, are the ones to share in the first resurrection. Implied is a second resurrection which would occur at the last judgment (Mt 25:31-46).

20:7-10 We are given the threat of the loosing of Satan from the bottomless pit, but then he is *thrown into the lake of fire* (v. 10) to join the sea beast and the false prophet (R). We have depicted a final battle where the forces of evil will be definitively conquered, and all humanity will attest to that fact. The forces of evil will be impotent before the Lord. The reference to Gog and Magog refers to Ezk cc. 38-39. However, there it is only Gog from the land of Magog (Ezk 38:2). Our author has made of one individual two people. Gog from Magog is a mythical person from a mythical country. No such place is to be found on the maps of the ancient world. It is a symbol for the nations who follow the great deceiver. However, they are powerless before the King of kings. The saints already dwell in the *beloved city* (v. 9); they are ruling with Christ now (v. 6). The *beloved city* is the *heavenly Jerusalem* (Heb 12:22).

20:11-15 The final judgment scene is depicted. The deeds of all people follow after them (14:13). The *book of life* and other books are opened. It does make some difference what one believes and how one lives. Judgment depends on that. Death and Hades were presented as humanity's enemies (6:8). Now in this judgment, they are powerless over the faithful. In fact, Death and Hades have been personified and are cast into *the lake of fire*, the final condemnation from which there is no reprieve. The *book of life* (v. 15) and the books of deeds (v. 12) are the basis for either the judgment of condemnation or the judgment of resurrectional life. Those in heaven are they who *have washed their robes and made them white in the blood of the Lamb* (7:14). John reminds his readers that faith is not merely intellectual—it has to be lived.

CHAPTER 21

A NEW HEAVEN AND A NEW EARTH

21:1-5 We are informed that paradise has been regained (P). In fact, cc. 21-22 form an antithesis with Gn cc. 1-3. In Gn 1-3, paradise had been lost; in Rv 21-22, we encounter paradise regained. There is a new creation; *for the first heaven and the first earth had passed away, and the sea was no more.* A beast had come from the sea (13:1). In heaven, no harm can come to the individuals who have safely arrived at their permanent home. There is a new world which has arrived (Is 65:17-19). This *new Jerusalem* is not the earthly city of Jerusalem. It is new; it is God's very special city. It is the people of God, born from the victorious life, who are espoused to the Lamb (19:9). God's dwelling is with his people (Ezk 37:27). The explanation of 7:15-17 has found its total fulfillment in our passage; God is with his people and there will no longer be any tears or crying or pain. Our author has depicted life here upon earth as a vale of tears. In heaven, *God himself will be with his people; he will wipe away every tear from their eyes.*

21:5-8 We are informed of a new creation. *Behold, I make all things new*(v. 5). *And God saw everything that he had made, and behold, it was very good* (Gn 1:31). *In the beginning God created the heavens and the earth* (Gn 1:1). After each of God's creative utterances, Genesis says: *And so it happened* (Gn 1:7). In our verses God says: *It is done* (v.6). God himself is called the *Alpha and the Omega*, the same words used of the Christ/Son of Man/

Lamb (22:13). The same title is used of God and of Christ, and thus indirectly points out the divinity of Christ. Water was a priceless commodity in the days of the Bible, most precious to be sure. In heaven, there will be free water, a *fountain of the water of life without payment*. The same expression is found in Jn 4:14 to indicate the abundance of life in the Spirit. No longer will God be related only to the people as such. Rather, in heaven he will be related to each individual: *I will be his God and he shall be my son*. Those who do not repent will not share in the new creation. Their lot shall be *the second death* in *the lake of fire*, i.e., condemnation with the beast and false prophet (19:20) and the devil (20:10).

21:9-14   The description of the bridegroom begun in v. 2 continues. *The holy city Jerusalem* is shown coming down out of heaven from God. God is uniting heaven and earth with this imagery of the holy city. The city recapitulates all the history of God's people, for the names of the *twelve tribes* are inscribed on the city gates and the names of *the twelve apostles of the Lamb* are inscribed on the foundations of the city. Both the old and the new people of God are joined together in this holy city. The jasper (4:3) and crystal (4:6) of God's throne room are found in this new city. The twenty-four elders (4:10) were said to represent the whole of God's people, of both the old and new covenants. The twelve tribes were specifically mentioned in c. 7. We have a picture of the Church, whose one solid foundation is Christ the Lamb.

21:15-21   We see the beauty of this heavenly city which is coming to join the earth. It is so big that only an angel can measure it. In c. 11, John was told to measure the temple; here an angel has to do the measuring. The measurements of the city are symbolic, containing multiples of the number twelve: a perfect city (F). In heaven there will be no ordinary building materials such as sandstone or limestone, just precious and semi-precious stones. This heavenly city is utterly magnificent, and there is nothing on earth to match it. *The twelve gates were twelve pearls* is the citation from which we derive "the pearly gates" of heaven. *The street of the city was pure gold*; the description is intended to boggle the mind.

21:22-27 We are told of the glory of the city. No temple is needed, since all sacrifice has ceased in heaven. The temple had been the place where God dwelled. In heaven, there is a direct meeting with *the Lord God the Almighty and the Lamb*. Thus, there is *no need of sun or moon*: God and the Lamb give off plenty of light. The *kings of the earth* are still given the chance to enter into the heavenly city. It is a free and safe city; for the *gates will never be shut*. Yet only those whose names are *written in the Lamb's book of life* can enter and find safety.

CHAPTER 22

REVELATION ENDS

22:1-5 The thought pattern of c. 21 is continued. The *river of the water of life* is reminiscent of the river which flowed through the garden of Eden in the first paradise (Gn 2:10). The same can be said of *the tree of life*; Adam and Eve ate of *the tree of knowledge of good and evil* (Gn 2:17), for they wanted to become *like God* (Gn 3:5). Eating of that tree caused death, not life. However, the *tree of life* is *on either side of the river* in the heavenly Jerusalem and with the abundant fruit coming twelve times a year from these trees, there healing and life are bestowed. We are told that even the nations can be healed by its leaves (v. 2). There is still held out to Christ's enemies the possibility of healing if they desire to be healed. Those in the heavenly city have the names of God and the Lamb upon them: they belong to God and to the Lamb. *And they shall reign for ever and ever*. Indeed, *the kingdom of the world has become the kingdom of our Lord and of his Christ, and he shall reign for ever and ever* (11:15). Those in the new Jerusalem reign with him.

22:6-7 Here begins a section dealing with threats and exhortations. It was common for the people of ancient times to change that which someone else had written. To counteract such a trend, apocalyptic writers often added threats to the end of their works. Our author is no exception. A prophet is one who speaks in God's behalf. *To show his servants what must soon take place* is an almost identical repetition of 1:1. *Blessed is he who keeps the words of the prophecy of this book* is parallel to 1:3.

22:8-11 We are dealing here with the worship of angels. Christians are not to worship angels, but the Lord alone. 19:10 dealt with the same subject matter. God's word was about to be fulfilled in the time of the writing of this Book: therefore, the message was to be an open message for all to read, and not a message sealed until the end of time (Dn 12:4).

22:12-16 These verses recapitulate many of the promises made at the beginning of the Book. Verse 13 paraphrases 1:8, 17. Verse 14 is the last of the seven beatitudes, and runs parallel with 7:14. *Root and offspring of David* corresponds to 5:5; the *tree of life* to 2:7; the *morning star* to 2:28. The promises held out to the faithful in the first part of the Book are fulfilled in the last two chapters.

22:17-21 Revelation is brought to a close with a note of hope and longing. The *Spirit* is *the spirit of prophecy* which is the *testimony of Jesus* (19:10). The *Bride* is the Church (19:7). Thus it is the Church and the members that cry out, *Come*. All who desire nourishment are asked to come to the Lord. He has *the water of life without price* for all those who come. Verse 18 is a warning against anyone who would alter what the author had written. As explained previously, this was common in ancient days. What we have is part of the literary form, the way of writing of the ancients; a curse was leveled on anyone who would dare change the author's message or writing. Of course, the curse only applies to Revelation, and not to the whole Bible. Each book was written separately, and all twenty-seven books of the NT were not put together until the end of the second century A.D.

The early Christians looked forward to the Lord's coming, and the Lord had promised that he would *come soon* to set things right. He did so by the Christians' conquest of the Roman Empire by the shedding of their blood, which led to the growth of the Christian community. The prayer of the early Christians is the same prayer which we utter today: *Amen, Come, Lord Jesus*: come into our lives now and set things straight. We wait patiently with anticipation for the final coming of the Lord, when he will take us by the hand and lead us into that heavenly city. In the meantime, we know that he comes to us each day to give us the strength and courage to live as people dedicated to the living God and his Son, Jesus Christ.

PART III

APPENDICES

HOW TO TEACH REVELATION

Drawing upon my own experience of teaching Revelation for twelve years to seminarians, priests, deacons, sisters and brothers, I have found it very useful to involve the students as much as possible in the learning experience. This involvement has taken various dimensions.

To truly appreciate the work, it becomes necessary to attempt some visualization of the visions which are encountered. I ask my students to do some artistic representations of a given vision, e.g., the inaugural vision of 1:12-20 or the heavenly throne room of cc. 4-5. The students are asked to use different colors and to be creative in drawing the given vision. When they have completed this project, either during class or at home, together with the class I try to explain what each student has depicted with his/her help. The purpose of doing this is to show the class that each vision has many dimensions, and that just one artistic rendition does not suffice to capture the depth and the breadth of the sacred author. The visions fade in and out, and any one picture is but one phase of that fading and focusing process. The student quickly learns that there is not just one fixed way of looking at each item in Revelation.

It is also necessary to use the voice in making the Book come alive. For this reason, it is necessary to use a common translation of Revelation for the purpose of choral recitation. Many of the hymns can be chorally recited, e.g., 5:9-14 is a prime example. One can divide the class into various sections to read parts of the hymn. A narrator would begin v. 9, one group would join the hymn in 9b, the narrator would read v. 11, and another group would join the first in chorally reciting v. 12b. The narrator would continue with v. 13, a third group would join the first two groups in reciting v. 13b, and the narrator would read v. 14 with the exception of the

Amen—which can be turned into a triple *Amen*, recited by the whole class.

To understand the Book, music is important as well. I often have my students play rhythm band instruments, whether professional or homemade, to accompany certain parts of a recitation. In this way, they can actually hear the Book and what it is saying. A good example of this would be 11:19, where various instruments can accompany the words *flashes of lightning and peals of thunder, an earthquake, and heavy hail*. The larger choral recitations can have different sounds joined to them: percussion, bells, wood sticks, maraca-like instruments. This is especially effective in the poetic laments of c. 18 and the hallelujahs of c. 19.

Also, one can capture the mood of Revelation by listening to music which flows directly from it. This can include not only the classical and modern pieces mentioned in Appendix II, but also rock and roll, country and western, jazz, new wave, and rhythm and blues. It is necessary for the teacher and the students to exercise their creative talents in this regard.

Movement, too, is important. At times, dramatic gestures should be employed in order to gather the full dimensions of what the author is expressing. 8:13 is a fine example. This verse lends itself to the teacher and students standing to recite and move their arms in a hovering position, in a lethargic way saying *Woe, woe, woe to those who dwell on the earth*.

Revelation will only be appreciated when the senses, as well as the intellect, are allowed to bathe themselves in the richness of God's inspired word. It is only in this way that one can really come to grasp what *apocalyptic* really means. Artists, poets, and musicians have always understood Revelation. Too often theologians have not, for they did not allow the senses to take part in the experience.

APPENDIX II

RESOURCES

The following works are listed so that one can do some further study of Revelation. Yet each of the books is not listed for the same reason. After each book, there is a brief description of why it is on the list. By listing these books, the present author does not want to give the impression that he agrees with everything that is found in these writings. This is in no way an exhaustive listing.

Ashcroft, Morris. "Revelation." Vol. 12 of the *Broadman Bible Commentary*. Broadman Press, 1972.

The commentary is filled with much useful information and makes application for the everyday life of the reader. Includes much spiritual content.

Coleman, Robert. *Songs of Heaven*. Fleming H. Revell Co., 1980.

A beautiful treatment of the various hymns found in Revelation. Each chapter is illustrated with a story from church life.

Collins, Adela Yarbro. *The Apocalypse*. Michael Glazier Press, 1979.

A straightforward and simple Catholic commentary useful for the laity.

Corsini, Eugenio. *The Apocalypse*, trans. Francis Moloney. Michael Glazier Press, 1982.

Commissioned by the Italian Episcopal Conference and first published in 1980. The author offers a practical and spiritual approach to Revelation.

Crane, Thomas. *The Message of St. John*. Alba House, 1980.

At the end of each chapter, there is a listing of study guides and questions useful for home Bible study groups.

D'Aragon, Jean-Louis. "The Apocalypse," *Jerome Biblical Commentary*. Prentice-Hall, 1968.

Useful for a once-over-lightly treatment of Revelation. Compact and to the point. Serviceable for those who already know something about Revelation.

Harrington, Wilfrid. *Understanding the Apocalypse*. Corpus Publications, 1969.

One of the most complete and still readable commentaries for the laity yet to be published. Highly recommended.

Heidt, William. *The Book of the Apocalypse*. Liturgical Press, 1962.

A useful pamphlet with much detail. A beginner's tool in the study of Revelation.

Kallas, James. *Revelation: God and Satan in the Apocalypse*. Augsburg Publishing House, 1973.

The author confronts the basic questions proposed: God and Satan, Millennium, Eastern thought patterns, historical situation and other issues. Highly recommended.

Massyngberde-Ford, Josephine. *Revelation*. Doubleday and Co., 1975.

Useful for word study, exegesis and detail. Scholarly.

Russell, D.S. *Apocalyptic: Ancient and Modern*. Fortress Press, 1978.

An excellent popular approach dealing with the true nature of apocalyptic.

Schick, Edwin. *Revelation: The Last Book of the Bible*. Fortress Press, 1978.

A quick overview of the Book, suitable for Bible study classes.

OTHER RESOURCES

The Cloisters Apocalypse. New York Metropolitan Museum of Art, 1971.

An early fourteenth century manuscript of the pictures and text of the Apocalypse has been reproduced. Excellent for appreciating the Apocalypse in art.

The Messiah by George Frederick Handel.

An oratorio written in 1742 and performed on March 23, 1743.

Especially to be noted in this composition is the *Hallelujah Chorus* at the conclusion of Part II and *Worthy Is The Lamb* at the conclusion of Part III. Excellent for appreciation of the Apocalypse in classical music.

Sancta Civitas by Ralph Vaughn Williams.

Composed between 1923 and 1925, it was first performed on May 7, 1926. It captures the ethereal mood of the heavenly Jerusalem. Useful in appreciating the Apocalypse in modern music.

Apocalypse: Part One: John's Vision by R. Murray Schafer.

A contemporary music-theatre work available through Arcana Editions, Bancroft, Canada. Composed for amateur musicians to be performed in music-theatre. For the musically gifted students of the Apocalypse.

Victory of Life by Erik Routley, 1975.

An interpretation of the Book of Revelation arranged for dramatic reading with congregational participation. Published in *Reformed Liturgy and Music*, Vol XII, Winter 1978. Excellent for choral interpretation of Revelation in a contemporary setting.

Savickas, Alfonsas. *The Concept of Symbol in the Psychology of C.G. Jung*. Resch Verlag Innsbruck, 1979.

An appreciation for symbols in religious and secular thought. Helpful in discovering insights into the visions of Revelation.